藏密本尊

Satyadevatas in Tibetan Esoteric Buddhism

汉英对照

The Chinese-English

索南才让 ◎著

顾毳 ◎译

陕西师範大學出版总社

Preface 前言

前言
Preface

藏密，是藏传佛教密宗的简称。藏密由印度传入，但却不是印度密教的简单移植，而是佛教文化和本土宗教文化相互碰撞、吸收融合的结果，是藏传佛教的重要一部分和藏族传统文化的精髓，具有非常鲜明的民族特色。佛教传入西藏的时间晚于汉地六百年左右，传说雅隆悉补野部落联盟第二十八代首领拉脱脱日年赞执政时期，从天降下《佛说大乘庄严宝王经》《百拜忏悔经》《六字大明陀罗尼》等佛教经典，它们都是密教莲花部的根本经典。由于当时没有人知道其中的内容，所以它们被作为“圣秘玄物”供放在王宫里面。公元七世纪吞米桑布扎创制藏文后，这些经典才被翻译成藏文，成为最早传入西藏的密教经典。八至九世纪，吐蕃王朝赤松德赞、赤德松赞、赤祖德赞“祖孙三王”在执政期间，组织翻译了包括事部、行部、瑜伽部、无上瑜伽部方面的大量经典和大圆满密法中的经典。十一至十三世纪期间，早期翻译的大圆满密法经过与苯教百余年的相互吸收融合，并且与民间社会的民俗生活相结合，基本形成体系。这一时期，被称为金刚乘密法中最高法门的无上瑜伽部的集密类、大威德类、喜金刚类、胜乐类、时轮类的经典和思想全部被译介进来，经过不断的诠释，系统的思想

The Tibetan Esoteric Buddhism, an important part of Tibetan Buddhism and a kernel of Tibetan culture, is not simply colonized from Indian Esoteric Buddhism but is the outcome of collision and integration between Indian Esoteric Buddhism and native Tibetan religious culture. The initial Buddhism spreading to Tibet was later than to Han Buddhism for almost six hundred years. A legend says that when Lha-THo-Tho-Ri-gNYan-bTSan, the twenty-eight generation of king of the Union of Tribes of Yar-Klungs-sPur-rGyal, ruled the biggest union in Tibet, three books fell down from the sky, which were *The Sutra of Ornament of the mahayana of the Great King, The Sutra of Hundreds Kowtow and Penitence,* and *The Six-Syllable Tantra*. These sutras are the basic sutras in the Padma Family of Esoteric Buddhism. In that time, because no one can read and understand these books, Tibetans regarded them as mysterious holy items and worshiped them in the palace. They were not translated until the seventh century when THon-Mi-Sam-BHo-Ta, an administrator of Srong-bTSan-sGam-Po, created Tibetan written language and translated them and found that these books were Esoteric Buddhism sutras. In the Eighth and Ninth century,KHri-Srong-lDe-bTSan,KHri-lDe-Srong-bTSan and KHri-gTSHug-lDe-bTSan organized the translation of massive Esoteric Buddhism sutras, including Kriyatantra, Charyatantra, Yogacharya, Anuttara Yoga Tantra, and Mahasampanna. During the eleventh to thirteenth century, these translations developed and integrated with the Bon Religion and folk customs. Finally, Tibetan Esoteric Buddhis formed its own system. With several centuries' endeavor, the highest Esoteric Buddhism sutras and thoughts of Vajrayana, such as the Secrets of Vairochana, Yamantaka, Hevajra, Samvara and Kalacakra, were all introduced to Tibet. With continuous interpretation of these sutras and thoughts, Tibetan Buddhist formed

理论、规范的修持方法、严格的师承关系和名目繁多而有等级差别的“神灵”体系得以产生，出现了以大圆满、一六明点、道果教授、大手印、六支瑜伽为核心密法的宁玛派、噶当派、萨迦派、噶举派、觉囊派，标志着藏传佛教密宗的正式形成。

在佛教创立发展的早期，信众在修行过程中不依赖任何神祇求得解脱，但随着印度佛教密教化趋势的加快，信众有选择地接纳婆罗门教、印度教和其他民间宗教的神祇作为护法神，如大黑天、马头金刚、不动明王、吉祥天母等，同时根据婆罗门教一些神祇的形象创造出如时轮金刚、胜乐金刚、喜金刚、集密金刚、大威德金刚等本尊，赋予他们新的内涵、名称及职责。这些印度密教本尊传入西藏后，面对强大的苯教神灵，藏人接受时，用苯教的神灵比附印度密教本尊进行改造，形成独特的藏传佛教本尊。如念青唐古拉山山神被解释成为密教金刚手菩萨的精魂，长寿五姐妹分别成为密教的空行佛母、金刚空行母、宝空行母、莲花空行母、业力空行母。在噶举派中，又有不动金刚吉祥佛母、金刚忿怒母、金刚笑母、金刚天女受用母、金刚舞女等密号。在庞大的护法神、本尊世界中，按照中国西藏和印度的神话谱系，他们每一位都有自己的形象、地位、

its own Esoteric Buddhism theory, ritual, the way of practice, the strict lineage system and the ranks of deities. Meanwhile, Nyingma School, Kadam School, Sakya School, Kagyu School and Jonangpa School also emerged. The central way of practice of these schools are Mahasampanna, Sixteen Bindus, Margaphala, Mahamudra and Six-branch Yoga, respectively. Above all, after the appearance of these schools, the special Tibetan Esoteric Buddhism generated and formed its special characteristics which are different from Indian Esoteric Buddhism and Han Esoteric Buddhism.

In the early time of Buddhism, Buddhists did their religious practice without relying on any deities. With the development of Esoteric Buddhism, Buddhism selectively accepted the deities of Brahmanism, Hinduism and other folk religions, such as Mahakala, Hayagriva, Acala and Lakshmi. According to the image of Brahmanism, Buddhism also created some deities as their Satyadevatas, such as Kalacakra Vajra, Cakrasamvara, Hevajra, Guhyasamaja, Vajrabhairava and endowed them new meanings, names and responsibilities. When Buddhism spread into Tibet, they faced the powerful deities of Bon. Buddhists compared their deities to Bon's, while in the same time changed Bon's deities into Buddhist dharma protectors. For example, the Bon's Deity of Nyenchen Tanglha Mountain is called the Spirit of Vajrapani in Tantra of Tibetan Buddhism, the Deities of Five Longevous Sisters, are called Dakini, Vajra Dakini, Ratna Dakini, Padma Dakini, Karma Dakini. They are alsonamed Acala Lakshmi, Vajra Krodhikali, Vajrahasa Mother, Vajra Devakanya Sambhogakaya Mother, Vajranrityani in Kagyu School. According to Tibetan of China and Indian myth, every Satyadevata and dharma protector has its own role, duty, and vivid image with clear ranks, some of them are clam and beautiful, some of them are fierce and horrible.

胎藏界曼荼罗

Garbhadhatu Mandala

职责等，主次分明，静怒有别，特征鲜明。

藏密重在事相，重视超自然、神话、仪式等，强化了本尊与护法神的作用，把佛、菩萨看成是祥和的宇宙精神体。修行者对佛、菩萨以及护法神的供养就是对这个宇宙精神体的精神信息能量的供养。

曼荼罗（坛城），藏文为 DKyil-' KHor，表现为密教本尊的道场和佛的宫殿，指一切的语言、声音、文字、名称等，是体相用一体的具体化，表示宇宙本身的全体相，是真理的符号化表现。“曼荼”，即本质；“罗”，是成就义，它的本来意思是圆轮、发生、精醇、聚集等，即圆轮众德、圆轮具足、发生诸佛，是佛陀自觉的境界。《喜金刚本续》说：“曼荼罗者，是心取大乐，菩提心即是大乐。”《大日经》说：“曼荼罗，即心圆满。”《时轮根本续》说：“曼荼罗者，法界也，法界大乐宫即是曼荼罗。”曼荼罗又是法的具象代表，是变化多样的神界结构，形式表现为本尊主神的聚会处。有印度文化专家说：曼荼罗本来是古印度时人们用来盛放供神食品的圆盘，后来逐渐演变成为一种传法时尤其授灌顶时必须建造的坛城，以防止外面的妖魔侵害。它在藏传佛教里不仅作传授灌顶的场所

Featured by the supernatural, mysterious and ritual, Tibetan Esoteric Buddhism focuses on phenomena and consolidates the role of Satyadevatas and dharma protectors. They consist of the holographic and harmonious spirit of the universe. Yogis do their worship to Buddhas, Bodhisattvas and dharma protectors as to the spiritual power.

Mandala, the room of Satyadevata, the palace of Buddha, and the world, means language, sound, word and name, is the body of substance, characteristic and function, is the whole phenomena of the universe itself and the symbolized truth. “Manda” means essence. And the original meaning of “la” refers to a circle, generation, purity and collection; extended meaning refers to achievement, completeness and perfection, the state of Buddhas. In *Hevajra Fundamental Tantra*, it is said that Mandala means the happiest, then Bodhichitta is the happiest. *Mahavairochana Sutra* (*Sutra of the Great Radiant One*) mentions that Mandala is the feeling of harmony and happiness. *Kalacakra Mulagrantha Tantra* says that Mandala is the world of Dharma; the big happy palace of Dharma is Mandala. Therefore, mandala is the body of dharma, is the structures of various worlds of deities. Mandala is the palace for deities to get together. An expert of Indian culture once said that, in ancient India, Mandala was a round plate used to worship, and then it gradually became an altar for the ceremony of teaching dharma and abhisheka in order to fend off the demons. In Tibetan Buddhism, Mandala is not only the room of abhisheka, but also regarded as religious ritual implements, called Tan City or DKyil-' KHor.

Generally, Mandala can be divided into Maha Mandala,

用，而且也作法器用。

一般曼荼罗分为大曼荼罗、三昧耶曼荼罗、法曼荼罗、羯磨曼荼罗四种，其中大曼荼罗描绘佛、菩萨的形象，三昧耶曼荼罗描绘象征佛、菩萨的器杖和印契，法曼荼罗表示诸佛、菩萨的种子，羯磨曼荼罗描绘佛、菩萨的威仪事业。每一种又各有都会（诸尊聚集）、部会（部分诸尊）、别会（一尊为主）曼荼罗。唐密重视根据《大日经》和《金刚顶经》绘制的胎藏界曼荼罗和金刚界曼荼罗。在形态上，唐密曼荼罗和藏密曼荼罗有相当大的差异性。唐密胎藏界曼荼罗中央有中台八叶莲花院；东部（上部）有遍知院、释迦院、文殊院；南部有金刚手院、除盖障院；西部有持明院、虚空藏院、苏悉地院；北部有观音院、地藏院。四方以外金刚部院为外围。金刚界曼荼罗与胎藏界曼荼罗在构造上有所不同，它的东方在下部，本尊面朝东，由如来部、金刚部、宝部、法部和羯磨部构成，分别配置在中央与四方：中央是大日如来佛，东方是不动金刚佛，南方是宝生佛，西方是阿弥陀佛，北方是不空成就佛。主要诸尊有三十七尊，故称金刚界三十七尊。

Samaya Mandala, Dharma Mandala and Karma Mandala. Among them, Maha Mandala paints the images of Buddhas or Bodhisattvas; Samaya Mandala depicts the symbolic religious ritual implements and mudra (or gesture and seal) of Buddhas and Bodhisattvas; Dharma Mandala is described as the seeds of Buddhas and Bodhisattvas and Karma Mandala is the Buddhas and Bodhisattvas' great enterprise. Every Mandala has three kinds: plenary meeting, partial meeting and sole meeting. According to the *Mahavairochana Sutra* and the *Vajrashekhara Sutra*, Tang Tantra focuses on the Garbhadhatu Mandala and Vajradhatu Mandala. There are enormous differences in form between Tang Tantra and Tibet Tantra. In Garbhadhatu Mandala of the Mandala of Tang Tanta, there are Eight-leaves Lotus Yard in the centre, Universal Knowledge Yard, Shakya Yard, Manjushri Yard in the east, Vajrapani Yard and Sarvanivara Naviskambini Yard in the south, Vidyadhara Yard, Akashagarbha Yard and Susiddhi Yard in the west an Avalokitesvara Yard and Kshitigarbha Yard in the north with the Thunderbolt Class Yard around. The structure of Vajradhatu Mandala is different from Garbhadhatu Mandala. The east of Vajradhatu Mandala is on the bottom, its Satyadevatas face to the east, including Buddha Family, Vajra Family, Treasure Family, Dharma Family and Karma Family. Mahavairochana Buddha is in the centre of the Garbhadhatu Mandala, Akshobhya Buddha in the east, Ratnasambhava Buddha in the south, Amitabha Buddha in the west, Amoghasiddhi Buddha in the north. There are altogether thirty-seven Satyadevatas in the centre and four directions respectively, so they are called Vajradhatu Thirty-seven Satyadevatas.

真实意

Truthful Mind

不同法门的藏密曼荼罗，其构造不尽相同，通常由圆轮构成，有立体和平面两种曼荼罗。立体曼荼罗多为金属和木材制作，平面曼荼罗有彩绘、唐卡、壁画和彩砂粉浮雕等。一般曼荼罗周围是金刚环，上方是金刚笼，下方是金刚地，在金刚地上面构筑楼阁，成为立体图像。莲瓣环绕在金刚环内侧，火轮在金刚环外侧，火轮颜色有分别代表地、水、火、风的黄、绿、红、蓝四色。根据所修的法，曼荼罗中央供不同的本尊，如佛、菩萨和时轮金刚、胜乐金刚、喜金刚、集密金刚、大威德金刚等，形象各异，有善相本尊、怒相本尊，也有善怒相兼的本尊，外围有菩萨、护法神等。

本尊藏语名为 Yi-Dam，“Yi”是“心意”的意思；“Dam”意为“圣贤”或“真理”。藏密各派都有自己主供的本尊和护法。宁玛派被看成是最具地方特色的宗派，它广泛吸收苯教的神祇为护法神，以普贤佛为修行追求的最高目标，达到修行者与普贤佛合而为一。它供奉的是八大法行中的出世法行的真实意、金刚橛、甘露功德、莲花语等。

噶举派以大手印法为核心，吸收《胜乐根本续》和《集

The dharma sects of Mandalas in Tantra of Tibetan Buddhism vary in structure. Commonly, Mandalas are circle and have two forms: three-dimensional and two-dimensional. The former are mostly made of wood and iron. The latter have various forms, such as painting, tangka, wall painting, chromatic sand relief. There are many vajra circles surrounding a mandala. And on the head of mandala there is a vajra cage. Castles and buildings are drawn as three-dimensional paintings on the vajra floor with vajra circles around. On the vajra circles, lotus' leaves are sculptured and fire wheels are painted. Fire wheels are yellow, green, red and blue symbolizing earth, water, fire, and wind. Practicing different dharma should make offerings to corresponding Satyadevata in the centre of mandala. Bodhisattvas and dharma protectors stand around Satyadevata. The image of Satyadevatas, such as Buddhas, Bodhisattvas, Kalacakra Vajra, Cakrasamvara, Hevajra, Guhyasamaja, Vajrabhairava, are distinctive and vivid. Some of them are amiable, some of them are wrathful, and some are both amiable and wrathful.

Satyadevatas, the transformation of Buddhas and Bodhisattvas, are named “Yi-Dams” in Tibetan. “Yi” means mind and “Dam” means truth and saint. Every school of Tibetan Buddhism worships their own Satyadevatas and dharma protectors. Nyingma, the particular ethnic school absorbing Bon's protectors as their own, regards the achievement of being Samantabhadra Buddha as their highest goal that yogi and Samantabhadra Buddha combine into one. Yogis make truthful mind, vajrakilaka, sweet dew merits and lotus word as offerings, which are four of Eight Dharma Actions for attainment in lives outside the world.

密根本续》等无上瑜伽部密法，以胜乐金刚和集密金刚为本尊，所以在他们的寺院里有大量的胜乐金刚和集密金刚画像、塑像、雕像。萨迦派以《喜金刚本续》为根本经典，以其中的道果教授为核心法，以喜金刚为本尊。觉囊派以《时轮根本续》为本经，以时轮六支瑜伽为核心法门，以时轮金刚为本尊。格鲁派是藏传佛教中最后形成的一个宗派，它在修学方面坚持先显后密（先理论后实践）、止观双运的次第，以大威德金刚为本尊，同时重视学习集密和时轮教法，把集密金刚和时轮金刚也作为重要本尊供奉。

本书用图文并茂的形式详细介绍藏密中比较重要的本尊和护法神，即时轮金刚、胜乐金刚、喜金刚、集密金刚、大威德金刚五大本尊和马头金刚、大黑天、吉祥天母、金刚亥母、金刚手、金刚持等护法神。他们的形象各不相同，有善相、怒相和善怒相兼具的，如时轮金刚、胜乐金刚、集密金刚、喜金刚、金刚亥母、吉祥天母等既有善相，也有怒相，是善怒相兼具的形象；怒相本尊、护法神有大威德金刚、金刚橛、马头金刚、大黑天、金刚手等。由于藏传佛教的传统艺术分勉唐、钦孜、噶赤三大派别，每一派的画法、用料等不尽相同，因此出现了同一个本尊或护法神有不同形象的现象。

Mahamudra, or great gesture, the key dharma door of Kagyu School, adopted the mysteries of the esoteric sect of Supreme Yoga Tantra from *Samvara Fundamental Tantra* and *Guhyasamaja Fundamental Tantra*. Because of this, it is easy to see everywhere in Kagyu's monastery the pictures, sculptures and statues about Cakrasamvara and Guhyasamaja. Sakya School, taking *Hevajra Fundamental Tantra* as their fundamental classic, made Margaphala (or Lamdre) as their key approach and Hevajra as their Satyadevata. Jonangpa School regards *Kalacakra Fundamental Tantra* as ultimate classic and Kalacakra Six-branch Yoga as kernel approach and sees Kalacakra Vajra as their Satyadevata. As the last formed school in the history of Tibetan Buddhism, Geluk School persist in studying the exoteric teaching of Buddhism first, and then the esoteric teaching of Buddhism and in keeping the order of the Union of Shamatha and Vipashyana. Their Satyadevata is Vajrabhairava. Because they attach importance to the secrets of Vairochana and Kalacakra in the same time, they also worship Guhyasamaja and Kalacakra Vajra as their Satyadevata.

This book aims at to introduce some important Satyadevatas and protectors of Tibetan Buddhism with vivid pictures, including the Five Satyadevatas: Kalacakra Vajra, Cakrasamvara, Hevajra, Guhyasamaja, Vajrabhairava and the dharma protectors of Vajrabhairava, Vajrakilaka, Hayagriva, Mahakala, and Vajrapani, etc. Their images are diverse. Some of them are amiable, some wrathful, some both amiable and wrathful. Traditionally, there have been three Thangka schools: SMan-GHang-Lugs, MKHyen-bTSe' i-Lugs and SGar-bRis-Lugs, each of them having developed different ways to paint with different materials. That is why the same Satyadevatas and dharma protectors show different images.

金刚橛

Vajrakilaka

甘露功德

Sweet Dew Merits

莲花语

Lotus Word

目录
Catalogue

一

金刚持

Vajradhara

金刚持
Vajradhara

金刚持，亦译“持金刚”或“执金刚”。梵文为 Vajradhara，“Vajra”意为金刚杵，“dhara”意为“执持”。藏文为 RGyal-Ba-rDo-rJe-‘CHang（嘉瓦多杰羌）。有些文章将其看成是金刚手或金刚萨埵，实际上三者是完全不同的，金刚持被认为是释迦牟尼佛说密法时所现的身形，是佛三身中的报身佛、本初佛，尊为秘密教主，诸佛共主。

噶举派文献说：金刚持自己发心修炼，经过无数大劫，积聚了许多福德资粮后才成佛。之前，他在色究竟天得到了十方诸佛的灌顶，刹那间清除一切无明烦恼，成就法身、报身、化身。他是三界一体中的觉者，在众生中是法体，通过自己菩提心的形式，成为功德圆满的佛。其常见的形象是单身坐像，一面二臂，身呈蓝色，象征无限证悟心；头戴有多种珠宝的花冠，略向左倾；双目微闭，自然下视；双唇紧闭，安然慈祥；一副大耳环垂于双肩，颈挂项链，腕戴手镯，象征清净觉悟心；身披丝带，双臂相交于胸前，左手拿金刚铃，右手持金刚杵，象征方便智慧合一；脚脖佩钏，赤足跏趺于莲花座上。

Vajradhara, or RGyal-Ba-rDo-rJe-‘CHang in Tibetan and Thunderbolt-in-hand in English, is considered, by some people, to be Vajrasattva (or Diamond Being) and Vajrapani (or Holder of the Vajra). Actually, they are totally different. Vajradhara is Sambhogakaya and Adibuddha, which is the appearance shown by Buddha when he teaches Tantra, so Vajradhara is respected as Tantra Master, the common master of every Buddha.

According to the literature of Kagyu school, Vajradkara made up his mind to practice Buddhist control of mind and body. After performing numerous good deeds of blessed virtue in face of countless mahakalpas, his ignorance and worries disappeared all of a sudden, he got Abhisheka from the Buddhas from all directions in Akanishta and attained Dharmakaya, Sambhogakaya, and Nirmanakaya. It is said that Vajradhara is the enlightened one of Three Realms and the entity of dharma of all living beings. He became a perfect and meritorious Buddha by the form of his own Bodhi Mind. In a statue, Vajradhkara is usually seen as sitting on a lotus seat with crossed legs, has one face and two arms. He has blue skin which symbolizes the infinite enlightenment. He wears a flower crown with variety of jewelry and slightly left-leaning. He looks down and almost closes his eyes. His lips pressed together peacefully and kindly. Drooping big earrings to shoulders, the nice necklaces hanging his neck, bracelets on his wrisks, all of these adorments are symbol of pure consciousness. He is wearing ribbons as a clock. With his the left hand holding a Vajra Bell and his right hand taking a Vajra, he cross his arms in front of the chest, signifying that approach and wisdom integrate into one.

金刚持

Vajradhara

金刚持

Vajradhara

金刚持

Vajradhara

金刚持

Vajradhara

金刚持

Vajradhara

金刚持
Vajradhara

金刚持
Vajradhara

大轮金刚持曼荼罗

The Mandala of Mahācakra Vajradhara

金刚手
Vajrapani

金刚手，梵文为 Vajrapani，藏文为 Pyag-Na-rDo-rJe 或 Lag-Na-rDo-rJe。金刚手又称金刚手菩萨或金刚手大势至，是随侍如来佛的八大菩萨之一，另七大菩萨是文殊、观世音、地藏、除盖障、虚空藏、弥勒、普贤。金刚手具有八大殊胜，即大轮自在殊胜、具蓝衣护法殊胜、调伏四脐轮火殊胜、催碎金刚殊胜、乌紥雅猛咒殊胜、忿怒大鹏鸟殊胜、教规金刚手疗疾殊胜、巴瓦玛密决殊胜。他头戴五叶宝冠，长发披肩，上身袒露，下着裙裳，腰系一条宽帛带，面带微笑，左手紧握金刚杵，臀部微向侧扭。

Vajrapani, or Holder of the Vajra, and Pyag-Na-rDo-rJe or Lag-Na-rDo-rJe in Tibet, also been called Vajrapani Bodhisattva or Vajrapani Mahasthamaprapta, is one of Buddha's eight assistant Bodhisattvas, which include Manjushri, Avalokiteshvara, Vajrapani, Kshitigarbha, Sarvanivara Naviskambini, Akashagarbha, Samantabhadra, and Maitreya. He possesses eight great merits, the great merit of big wheel in nature, the great merit of possessing protective blue skin, the great merit of taming the fire on belly button, the great merit of destroying vajra, the great merit of u-za-ya tantra, the great merit of annoying Garuda Bird, the great merit of healing disease, the great merit of ba-wa-ma tips. He has long hair and wears five-leaves gold crown on his head and dresses in a colorful skirt with naked upper body. He always wears a smile and holds a Vajra in his hand. His buttock twist a little.

金刚手
Vajrapani

金刚萨埵

Vajrasattva

金刚萨埵，梵文为 Vajrasattva，意为“金刚众生”，藏文为 RDo-rJe-Sems-dPa‘。佛经对他是菩萨还是佛有不同的说法，藏密尊其为百部本尊之共主，归在菩萨之中。其形象有单身和双身两种，常见的是一面二臂单身像——面相圆浑，发髻高竖，右手于胸前持金刚杵，左手置脐下持金刚铃，全身珠宝装饰，坐在莲花宝座上。

Vajrasattva, Diamond Being in English and RDo-rJe-Sems-dPa‘ in Tibetan. There are different opinions as to whether Diamond Being is a Buddha or Bodhisattva. Tibetan Buddhism attributes Vajrasattva to a Bodhisattva as the master of hundreds of Satyadevatas. He appears in two forms: one is single-body and the other is double-body. The most commonly seen one is the single Diamond Being. He has a round face and two arms, his right hand holding the Vajra in front of his chest and left holding a Vajra Bell below belly button. He is adorned by jewelries and sits on a lotus seat.

金刚萨埵单身像

The Single-body Statue of Vajrasattva

金刚萨埵单身像

The Single-body
Statue of Vajrasattva

金刚萨埵单身像

The Single-body Statue of Vajrasattva

金刚萨埵双身像

The Double-body Statue of Vajrasattva

金刚萨埵双身像

The Double-body Statue of Vajrasattva

金刚萨埵曼荼罗

The Mandala of Vajrasattva

二

时轮金刚

Kalacakra Vajra

时轮金刚
Kalacakra Vajra

时轮金刚，既是藏密无上瑜伽部五大本尊之一，又是时轮教法的名称，梵文为 Kalacakra Vajra，藏文为 Dus-Kyi-‘KHor-Lo，意为“时间之轮”。“时间”即佛教所说的过去、现在、未来三时；“轮”是时间运行的规律或一种悟道的大乐经验，指生命和宇宙在时间中的生灭规律和与此相应的修炼方法，以及所要达到的终极目标。时轮从教法上分为外时轮、内时轮和别时轮。外时轮是指器世间，时间在此被看成是一个循环过程，一年四季，春夏秋冬，无始无终，流动不息，像轮子不停地转动，周而复始，形成四季的交替和万物的生灭。内时轮是指情世间，指人体的气、脉、明点的循环，形成人体的新陈代谢和生死轮回。别时轮是指灌顶、坛城、气、脉、明点等的修行方法，是针对外轮与内轮的对应规律，提出一个对策，主动控制，调整气脉，保精养神，成就空乐不二。

关于时轮教法的来源，传说是释迦牟尼圆满觉悟成佛的次年三月十五日，在南印度的灵鹫山讲《般若经》时，应香巴拉国月贤王与其九亿六千万城的眷属的祈求，在功德山附近一个叫吉祥聚米塔的宝塔的宝瓶里下化法界语自在，即圆满时轮金刚身、口、意曼荼罗的七百二十二尊佛，中化金刚界曼荼罗，上化吉祥星宿曼荼罗的一千六百二十

Kalacakra Vajra, Dus-Kyi-‘KHor-Lo in Tibetan and the wheel of Time in English, is not only one of five Satyadevatas in Supreme Yoga of Tibetan Esoteric Buddhism, but also the name of Kalacakra Teaching. The Buddhist conception of time refers to the past, the present and the future. The wheel is the law of time and its experience of awakened truth. So Kalacalra Vajra stands for the law of birth and death, the life and the universe in the time, the practice of the approach toward become Buddha and the ultimate goal of living beings. Kalacakra Teaching ccomprises of External Wheel of Time, Internal Wheel of Time and Other Wheel of Time. External Wheel of Time refers to the Realm of Matter, which regards time as a circle, running around again and again from spring, summer, autumn to winter, without a beginning and an end. Internal Wheel of Time, also the Realm of Feeling, indicates the circulation of the body's qi, meridians and bindu, which forms the metabolism and the circle of life. Other Wheel of Time refers to Abhisheka, mandala, qi, meridians, bindu and other ways of practice. In response to the law of External Wheel of time and the law of Internal Wheel of time, Other Wheel of Time presents countermeasures to control and adjust yogis' qi and meridians so as to keep practitioners' spirit and make them reach the union of emptiness and bliss.

The origin of Kalacakra Teaching can date back to the year following Shakyamuni Buddha's nirvana, when he was teaching Candrabhadra, the king of Shambala, and his people from his nine hundred and sixty million cities the *Wisdom Sutra* in the Gridhrakuta Mountain in the south of Hindustan. During the lecture, Shakyamuni Buddha, in a great treasure vase of the precious pagoda of Dhanakataka near Punyatara Mountain, enlightened the Language Ishvara of Dharmadhatu, seven hundred and twenty-two Buddhas statues in the Mandala of perfect Kalacakra Vajra's

大清乾隆年敬造

时轮金刚

Kalacakra Vajra

尊佛，传授世间法与出世间法的灌顶，宣讲无上瑜伽部的集密、胜乐、喜金刚等密法。佛陀自身化现为时轮本尊，用四首面的正面——意金刚之口宣讲以时轮金刚为主的无上瑜伽部密法，用左、右、后三面之口宣讲事部、行部、瑜伽部三部密法，当时无数的佛、菩萨、勇士、空行与天、龙、夜叉等一切人与非人都得到了自己所希望的成就。

松巴·益西班觉的《如意宝树史》说：“佛祖释迦牟尼正觉后的第二年，即时轮历的元年三月，在伐折罗波那南部吉祥聚米塔内大乐地，化现大曼荼罗，佛祖入定于吉祥时轮三摩地，向入坛眷属佛菩萨、请问者眷属香巴拉国日光王之子即金刚手的化身月贤王以及其他九十六王等众有缘者，宣讲《时轮根本续》一万二千颂。”

第五世达赖喇嘛的《西藏王臣记》中说：“岁次壬辰年三月十五日，于室利达那耶陀迦（即灵鹫山东面的吉祥聚米山），为护持一切秘密法藏的月贤法王宣说《吉祥最初佛时轮金刚根本续》，凡一万二千颂。月贤法王将该经迎请到藏拔拉（即香巴拉），于玛拉耶苑中，创建圆满具足佛陀身、语、意三密所依之大曼荼罗形象，智慧威光，赫赫有灵，幻舞游戏，变化多端，为迎请真实智慧尊而开

body, mouth and mind, the Vajradhatu Mandala andone thousand, six hundred and twenty Buddhas in the Mandala of Lucky Stars. Shakyamuni Buddha passed on the abhisheka of worldly dharma and out-of-worldly dharma, preached Guhyasamaja, Samvara, and Hevajra of Supreme Yoga Tantra. Transforming himself as Satyadevata of the Wheel of Time, Shakyamuni Buddha used the front side of his four faces heading toward different directions to explain Supreme Yoga Tantra and the other three faces to teach Performance Tantra, Action Tantra and Yogacharya Tantra respectively. Numerous listeners, such as buddhas, bodhisattvas, warriors, dakinis, devas, nagas and yakshas acquired the achievements they want.

Sum-Ba Ye-SHes-dPal- 'Byor said in his book, *the History of Kokonor* that on March of the first year of the Kalacakra calendar, also the second year of Buddha's sambodhi, Shakyamuni Buddha got in auspicious Kalacakra Samadhi and transformed a big Mandala in the great treasure vase of the precious pagoda of Dhanakataka in the southern Vajradharapona. In that time, The Buddha preached twelve thousand stanzas of *Kalacakra Fundamental Tantra* to Bodhisattvas, King Candrabhadra and other kings ruled by him.

According to *Records of Tibetan Kings and Ministers*, on fifteenth Martch, the next year of Buddha's nirvana, The Buddha made a spreach *the Fundamental Tantra of Kalacakra of Lucky First Buddha* to King Candrabhadra for upholding esoteric dharma. King Candrabhadra honorably brought the sutra to Shambhala and created the Great Mandala , which was lighting wisdom and sparking spirits changefully and magically for manifestng Buddha's

光庆祝，使迦罗波城（香巴拉国都城名）所有众生俱得共享金刚密乘的法缘。”

月贤王是日光和尊胜天女之子，他带着从佛那听闻的一万二千颂《时轮根本续》回到香巴拉后用文字记录下来，并作注疏，取名为《时轮金刚根本续广疏》，全书共有六万偈颂。次年，在一个叫玛拉耶的花园里，他用彩色宝石建造了一个时轮立体曼荼罗，讲时轮金刚密法。当王位传至第八代妙吉祥法王时，香巴拉国出现了四大种族，其中有些人信仰的是佛教之外的其他教（佛教称为外道），妙吉祥法王利用各种神通降伏了这些外道，统一了金刚种族，因此他又被称为第一代“具种法王”。传说香巴拉国有二十五代法胤，他们是金刚化身妙吉祥称、观世音菩萨化身白莲花、阎王化身佳善、地藏王菩萨化身尊胜、昏聩行化身善友、除盖障菩萨化身宝手、傲慢行化身遍入藏、虚空藏化身日称、除障明王化身极善、金刚手化身海胜、阎王化身难胜、地藏王菩萨化身太阳、昏聩行化身众色、除盖障菩萨化身月光、傲慢行化身天边、虚空藏化身护国、除障明王化身拥祥、金刚手化身狮子、阎王化身镇服、地藏王菩萨化身巨力、昏聩行化身不灭、除盖障菩萨化身人中狮王、虚空藏化身大自在天、除障明王化身天边尊胜、

mystic body, mouth and mind. The king also held an inauguration for inviting the truthful and intelligent aryas. Because of this, the Kalapa City the capital of Shamhbala, became a holy land of Dajra Vehicle.

King Candrabhadra, the son of Suryaprabha and Usnisavijaya wrote down twelve thousandstanzas of *Kalacakra Fundamental Tantra* taught by Buddha. He also compiled his own commentaries and wrote *the Wide Commentary on the Fundamental Tantra of Kalacakra Vajra*.The following year, he built a Kalacakra Mandala using colorful gemstones in the garden of Malaya for delivering lectures of Kalacakra Vajra Dharma. In the reign of Manjushri, the eighth king of Shambhala, there were four big races, some of them believing in non-Buddhist teachings. Manjushri King used various supernatural powers through mental concentration to have them at his feet and unified Vajra race. That is why he was also known as the first generation of "Bhyamyujyate Dharma King". It is said that the State of Shambhala carried on for twenty-five generations. When Sudurjayabhyamyujyate Dharma King, the eleventh Shambhala king, ruled, an Indian yogi named Maha Kalacakrapada, followed Satyadevata's prophecy to go to Shambhala to get dharma. On the way, he met the Sudurjayabhyamyujyate Dharma King's nirmanakaya who teached him Six-branch Yoga (or Successive Complete Kalacakra). It only took his six-month practice before reaching complete achievements. He used supernatural power to get to Shambhala and paid respect to the Sudurjayabhyamyujyate Dharma King. The king gave him *Kalacakra Fundamental Tantra* and *the Three Bodhisattva Commentary* and many tantra dharmas. He brought these tantras back to India.

时轮金刚
Kalacakra Vajra

时轮金刚

Kalacakra Vajra

妙金刚化身勇武轮王。代代相传至第十一代难胜具种法王时，有一位名叫大时轮足的印度瑜伽修炼者，根据所得到的本尊预言，前往香巴拉取法，途中遇到难胜具种法王的化身，听讲六支瑜伽（时轮圆满次第）法，只修了六个月就获得成就，即圆满殊胜悉地。他通过神通来到香巴拉，拜见难胜具种法王，得到《时轮根本续》《三菩萨释》等许多密宗续部的传承后，将一些经续和陀罗尼带回中印度。

多罗那他有类似的说法，他说清净圆满佛觉悟成道的第二年，在吉祥奥里萨的迦扎迦城大塔，化现吉祥星宿大曼荼罗，佛祖聚集其他佛、文殊菩萨、空行、十二大本尊、天、龙、夜叉，以及悉多河北部九亿六千万个村庄的有情众生，应金刚手化身月贤王请求讲授了包括《时轮根本续》在内的一切经续，使无数人、非人都得到成就。回到香巴拉国后，月贤王整理《时轮根本续殊胜最初佛》一万二千颂，并为之作注六万颂。天工巧匠以各种珠宝建造直径四百肘的曼荼罗。从此时轮教法在香巴拉传讲，历经几十代法王，逐渐传播开来，于公元十二世纪初传入西藏。

香巴拉，又译“香格里拉”，意为“持乐世界”或“持

Taranata has the similar saying that the year after the Buddha's nirvana, he transformed himself as Great Lucky Star Mandala and got together buddhas, Manjushri, dakinis, twelve great Satyadevatas, deities, demons and all living beings in nine hundred and sixty million villages near the north Sirtha River for preaching, upon the request of King Candrabhadra (the nirmanakaya of Vajrapani), *Kalacakra Fundamental Tantra* and every other tantras at the Kalapa Tower in lucky Orisa City, helping many listeners gained accomplishments. King Candrabhadra wrote down the twelve thousand stanzas of *the First Extraordinary Buddha Fundamental Tantra of Kalacakra* and also made a commentary on it. Craftsmen coming from the heaven built a mandala of four hundred inches in diameter with all kinds of jewels for delivering lectures to thousands of people. Since then, the Teaching of Kalacakra got spread out in Shambhala and was introduced, in the twelfth century, to Tibet.

Shambhala, also translated as Shangrila, means the World of Holding Happiness. It is the Sukhavati World in Buddhism and the original place of the teaching of Kalacakra. According to Tibetan *Kalacakra's Origin and Source*, Shambhala was a lotus-shaped valley enclosed in the central west of snow mountains. Between the snow cap on the top to the green grass at the foot spread many lakes and practice resorts. In the centre of the mountain top located twelve yojana Kalapa Palace, which centered the Sudurjayabhyamyujyate King's majestic and splendor throne. Around the palace distributes lots of ponds and at the south of the palace was the Malaya Garden which covered an area of twelve yojanas. In the middle of the garden is surrounded by Mandalas built by other kings, there was the almost one hundred thirty-seven meters high of tridimensional

安乐”，即佛教所说的净土世界，是时轮教法的发源地。根据藏文《时轮源流》描述，香巴拉位于雪山中央的西端，犹如莲瓣一样的圆形地域，被雪山环抱，从白雪皑皑的山顶到山下的绿地之间，大小湖泊星罗棋布，青草茂盛，绿树成荫，散布着许多修行圣地。中央的迦罗波宫殿，面积十二由旬，殿内中央有具种王的宝座，富丽堂皇。宫殿周围有着大大小小的池塘。宫殿南面的玛拉耶园林占地十二由旬，中央有月贤王用五色珠宝建造的高四百一十二尺的时轮身、语、意立体曼荼罗，周围耸立着其他诸王建的曼荼罗。园林东面有如意湖，西面有白莲湖。普通房舍都是两层建筑。具种王顶留发髻，呈五部佛相，头戴班智达帽，为转轮王相。

第六世班禅班丹益西的《香巴拉指南》这样描述：“这辽阔、浑圆的成就地，周围有皑皑的雪山环绕，西南面和东面均有可行走的道路。各雪山中间有茂密的檀香树林环绕，若将此浑圆之域平分为三等份，其似莲花的中心，坐落着噶拉巴（迦罗波）宫殿，周围被雪山和森林环绕，从宫殿到周围的山之间有五百由旬的距离。从山边森林沿雪山登上几天就能见到雪峰。峰顶因为是终年不化的积雪，已变成平展而闪闪发光的冰晶，噶拉巴就在此平阔的山

Kalacakra Mandala made up of the body, mouth and mind established by King Candrabhadra with five kinds of gemstones. In the east of the garden, there was the Wish-fulfilling Lake and the west, the White Lotus Lake. The King Sudurjayabhyamyujyate made his hair in a bun like five Buddhas' appearance and wore a pandita hat like a Cakravartin.

Pal-Den-Ye-SHe, the Sixth Panchen Erdeni describes in *the Guide to Shambhala* that this wide place of accomplishment was like a circle with white snow mountains around. On its two ends, there were paths leading toward the south-west and the east. Dense sandal woods divided the round place into three, the central part being the Kalapa Palace located in a lotus-shaped area surrounded by rings of snow mountains and forests. The distance between the palace and the mountains was more than five yojanas. If one had climbed the mountain from the edge of forest, he would have spent several days reaching the top. Because the snow never melt at the peak, it became flat and glittering ice crystal. In the middle of the ice crystal was Kalapa. This glorious palace was built by numerous jewelries which shined over a distance of one yojana. The radiance of palace and the snow mountains complement one another, making the place as bright as day even in the deep night and where one can even read books. The moon would become grey and lose its luminescence in comparison. Gyok-Lo-Sang-Don-Drup narrated in *the Biography of RGyal-dPal-Grags-Pa* that the moon cannot match the radiance of the palace, so it will escape on the excuse of travelling. In the palace, the bedroom of the King Sudurjayabhyamyujyate was made of emeralds, moon crystals, diamonds and other kinds of crystals. These shining jewelries make the night as bright as the day. King Sudurjayabhyamyujyate's golden throne was also imbedded with invaluable jewelries. They

时轮金刚

Kalacakra Vajra

顶。……这座壮丽的宫殿由各种无瑕之宝所建，其光芒照射近一个由旬的范围。此光辉与周围雪山峰顶之光交相辉映，使此地即使在深夜，也如阳光明媚的白昼，就连蝇头小楷也能阅读。若在此光明中观赏明月，月亮反呈淡淡的

were like mirrors reflecting images in fifty yojana. There was a crystal circle wheel in the surface of skylight through which one can see the sun, moon, stars and all the deities, gardens, planets and zodiac, as if these were really in front of you. With incense burners of santalum album placed around the golden throne, the aroma covered an area of one yojana radius. There were also

灰白色，显得没有一丝儿光泽。杰罗桑曲坚的《坚华扎巴传》形容说：‘月亮不敌其光辉，借口周游而逃遁。’在宫殿中，柔旦王（具种王）的卧室由子母绿宝石、月亮水晶、金刚石等各种宝石所造，因而闪闪发光乃至分不出昼夜来。柔旦王的上品金制宝座，也由各种宝石所镶嵌。这些无价之宝表面明亮如镜，从中可以观到五十由旬之内的水生动物的身影。天窗表面有一块水晶圆轮，从中可看到日、月、星辰，还有诸天、花园、行星、十二宫，等等，这一切仿佛都呈现在你的眼前。宝座的周边有白檀香护钳，香气远飘将近一个由旬。还有贵人所用的布和绸缎，价值黄金千万两的褥子、靠垫等，在此象征性地略述一二而已。总之，其居住的任何一处的价值都可与装满一座城池的黄金相比。”（索南才让著：《评介第六世班禅班丹益西的〈香巴拉指南〉》）

时轮金刚在密教里被看成是报身佛，他是释迦牟尼佛讲授密法时所化现的本尊，代表十方诸佛、菩萨以及显教和密教的总体，是真理的最完美显现。也说他是释迦牟尼佛说时轮法时所化现的威严相，象征时轮法的义理。

在藏传佛教的造像（唐卡画像）中，时轮金刚本尊有

fabulous textiles. Above all, the palace is the most rare and precise in the world.

Kalacakra Vajra is regarded as the Sambhogakaya Buddha who is the Satyadevata when Sakyamuni Buddha was teaching tantra and symbolized the Buddhas of ten directions, Bodhisattvas and the totality of the exoteric and esoteric Buddhism as well as the perfect embodiment of truth. Namely, the appearance transformed from Sakyamuni Buddha when he was teaching the Kalacakra Dharma's theory.

In Tibetan Buddhism, the paintings and sculptures of Kalacakra Vajra are usually presented as one body with two arms, one body with four arms, two bodies with many arms and so on. The most common one is the double-body statue: the Kalacakra Vajra Satyadevata hugging the Empty and Bliss Mahamudra Buddhamatri. Kalacakra Vajra Satyadevata wears blue heaven clothes (stands for "air"), tiger skin-made skirt and jewelry ornaments. His right leg is red (stands for "spirit") and left leg is white (stands for "blood") The air, spirit, and blood are the four fundamental components of life. From the aspect of External Wheel of Tim, red leg represents the Tropic of Cancer, the white leg means the Tropic of Capricorn. Kalacakra Vajra Satyadevata treads on the gods of Hinduism, the right leg being straight and treading on the red Desire god while the left bendings and treading on the Fear Demon. It signifies the conquering of desire, anger and ignorance.

Sometimes, Kalacakra Vajra has four heads and twelve arms. Every head has different color, the front one in black which

单身二臂、单身四臂和双身多臂几种形象。常见的是双身多臂像，即佛父时轮金刚拥抱大手印空乐佛母像。佛父时轮金刚上身穿着天衣，呈现蓝色，代表“气”；下身系虎皮裙，佩戴珠宝瓔珞，双腿颜色左白右红，分别代表精、血。精、气、血三种元素是生命的根本。从外时轮说，红色右腿代表北回归线，白色左腿代表南回归线。其双脚的站立姿势是，右腿向外伸直或侧直，左腿弯曲，微呈弓形。双脚踩踏印度教（湿婆教）的神衹阿难噶、鲁陀罗，也说右脚踩红色欲望神，左脚踩白色畏怖妖魔及其明妃拉提（欢爱天女）和高利（高利天女），表示制服贪、嗔等无明烦恼障。

佛父时轮金刚四头四面十二臂，四面颜色不同，前面蓝黑色，代表四大中之“风”；左面白色，代表“水”，呈寂静相；后面黄色，代表“土”，呈禅定表情；右面红色，代表“火”，表现出渴望的情态。风、水、土（地）、火构成宇宙的主要元素，分别代表着外时轮器世间的秋、夏、春、冬四季，也表示佛教的增益、息灾、敬爱、降伏四种事业，象征着功德圆满。四面的每一面各有三只眼睛，象征洞察一切。四头的每一头戴着五方佛骷髅冠，头顶半月和双金刚。十二臂代表一年十二个月，每臂又各有一只臂，共二十四只手臂，代表全年二十四个节气。手臂颜色为四双白色，

means wind, the right in red for fire (desire), the back head in yellow for earth (meditation), the left head is white for water (calmness). The wind, fire, earth and water are the main elements of the world which symbolize the four seasons (autumn, winter, spring and summer) of the Realm of Matter of External Wheel of Tim as well as the four enterprises of Buddhism (advancement, ending calamities and sufferings, love and taming), representing the completion of good deeds of blessed virtue. Every head wears a skull crown and put half-moon-like ornament and two vajra on these heads. Twelve arms mean twelve months. Every arm has a two forearm. The twenty-four forearms stand for twenty-four solar terms. The top eight are white, the middles are red and the bellows are blue. Every hand has five fingers which are yellow, white, red, blue and green respectively. Different color symbolizes the purity, clarity and awareness of the body, mouth and mind. Twenty-four hands have one hundred and twenty fingers. Every finger has three parts, which altogether constitute three hundred and sixty parts representing the three hundred and sixty days of a year. The right hands hold axe, cane, spear, wheel of dharma, hammer, drum of dharma, hook stick, arrow, knife, trident, sword and vajra respectively. The left hands take four-side head of Brahmadeva, chain, mirror, white conch, lotus, mani, rope, bow, skull, the drum of dharma, shield and vajra bell respectively. There are still other similar sayings.

In the famous Tibetan thangka on the main arms of Kalacakra Vajra grow two pairs of forearms from their elbows. The first pair embraces, in front of the bosom, Empty and Bliss Mahamudra Buddhamatri, with the left hand taking Vajra Bell and the right hand holding the vajra. The second pair is put in front of his belly, with the left hand taking a Dharma Wheel,

时轮金刚

Kalacakra Vajra

时轮金刚曼荼罗

The Mandala of Kalacakra Vajra

四双红色，四双蓝色，即上面八臂白色，中间八臂红色，下面八臂蓝色。每只手从拇指至小指的颜色依次是黄、白、红、蓝、绿。不同颜色的手臂象征清净和觉悟的身、语、意。每手五指，二十四只手有一百二十只手指，每指三节，共三百六十节，代表一年三百六十天。每只手持物，右手自上而下拿着钺斧、宝杖、矛、法轮、锤、法鼓、钩杖、箭、刀、三叉杖、宝剑、金刚杵，又说由上而下依次是金刚杵、宝剑、三叉戟、钺刀、火箭、钩杖、法鼓、锤、法轮、矛、宝杖、钺斧；左手从上至下依次持有四面梵天首、钩链、镜子、白海螺、白莲花、摩尼宝、绳索、弓、颅器、法鼓、盾牌、金刚铃，又说从下至上依次是金刚铃、盾牌、降魔杵、颅器、弓、绳索、摩尼宝、白莲花、白海螺、镜子、钩链、四面梵天首。

按照唐卡画像，时轮金刚主臂在肘关节处分出两对小臂：第一对小臂在胸前拥抱大手印空乐佛母，左手在里，拿着金刚铃，右手在外，持金刚杵；第二对小臂向下，左手握一法轮，右手执一宝剑。佛母身体呈现土黄色或红色，从外时轮讲象征太阳，散发七色光芒，代表有形有相的地气，她与佛父的蓝色代表的无形无相的天气（阳气）相合，表示色空相依，天地相合。从内时轮讲，空乐佛母的红色

the right hand holding a sword. Normally, Mahamudra's skin is earthy yellow (sometimes red). From the perspective of External Wheel of Tim, it symbolizes the shining sun and represents the tangible and visible earth air, and its combination with the intangible and invisible heaven air (Yang qi) of Kalacakra Vajra's blue skin becomes the symbol of the integration of materialness and emptiness and the heaven and the earth. From the angle of Inside Wheel of Time, the red color of Empty and Bliss Mahamudra Buddhamatri means blood and its integration with Kalacakra's blue face (means qi) represents their interdependence. Empty and Bliss Mahamudra Buddhamatri has four faces (sometimes two faces) three eyes and eight arms. The middle face is yellow, the left is red, the right is white and the face behind is blue. The four right hands are taking knife, hook stick, the drum of dharma and prayer beads respectively, while the four left hands are holding skull, rope, white lotus and mani treasure each.

Buddhamatri wears the buddhavamsa's clothes and ornaments of ancient India and stretches her left foot to embrace Kalacakra. In the eight-petal lotus-like lunisolar throne, the vajra and the colorful sands are the symbols of Kalacakra and Buddhamatri respectively. Sometimes, in the throne, there are five words: "A","Va", "Ra", "Ha", "Kha". "A" is yellow and means earth, "Va" is white and means water,"Ra" is red and means fire, "Ha" is green and means wind, "Kha" is blue and means empty. In the Kalacakra Mandala, those who always accompany Kalacakra Vajra and Empty and Bliss Mahamudra Buddhamatri are Amitabha and Prajna Buddhamatri, and blue Vajrasattva and his Vajradhatu Buddhamatri. Their symbol is a layer of sand under the Kalacakra Vajra and Empty and Bliss Mahamudra

代表人体内的“血”，与佛父时轮金刚的蓝色所代表的“气”相合，表示气血相依。佛母有四面八臂三目，四面的中间一面为黄色，左面为红色，右面为白色，后面为蓝色。八臂中右边四手持钺刀、钩杖、法鼓、念珠，左边四手持颅器、绳索、白莲花、摩尼宝。

佛母的身上穿戴有佛陀种姓的五印装饰，其左脚伸展，与时轮金刚交抱。时轮金刚以金刚杵为代表，空乐佛母以一层彩沙为代表，安居在八瓣莲花日月座的中心。有时莲花座从上到下有代表地、水、火、风、空五大字母，其中“阿”（A）字是黄色，代表“地”；“哇”（Va）字是白色，代表“水”；“啰”（Ra）字是红色，代表“火”；“诃”（Ha）字是绿色，代表“风”；“佉”（Kha）字是青色，代表“空”。在时轮曼荼罗中，与佛父佛母不可分离的是绿色的阿弥陀佛和般若佛母，以及蓝色的金刚萨埵及其金刚界佛母，以一层彩沙为代表安居在时轮金刚及其佛母下面。因此在莲花的中心就有六位本尊安住，莲花的八叶上安居着八位本尊，加上般若佛母和金刚界佛母，共有十尊，代表十波罗蜜多：布施、持戒、忍辱、精进、禅定、智慧、方便、愿、力、智。

Buddhamatri. So there are six Satyadevatas in the centre of the lotus throne, and eight Satyadevatas are settled on eight petals of the lotus respectively, together with Prajna Buddhamatri and Vajradhatu Buddhamatri, there are ten Satyadevatas, which reprent ten Paramitas, namely alms giving, Keep moral laws, patience under insult, pure progress, meditation, wisdom, skillful method, wishes, strength, knowledge.

The images of Kalacakra Vajra are presented in Tangkas, metal-made and medicine-clay-made statues and wall paintings, Which are colorful and vivid.

The mandala of Kalacakra Vajra takes the form of painting (such as Tangka and wall painting), of flat colorful sand, and of three-dimentional representation. According to relative records, the materials of painting are high quality and painters usually adopt five kinds of material. The painting brushes also use special material, such as rosewood, white sandalwood, person's bone, crow's tail, golden brush, dalbergia wood and auspicious wood and so on.

When building mandala the first thing is to choose the location and then make the lines. Facing east, an Acharya is sitting in a hero posture with thread in his left hand. His disciple sitting opposite him and the right hand holds thread. The shape of mandala is square in the middle of which the first Brahman line is drawn. Then, the Acharya turns to face south and the disciple to south. They begin to make the second Brahman line, wind-fire line and angular line. The next lines respectively draw from south to west, from north to east, from east to south, from west to north. Then, they need to draw ninety-six lines from the

时轮金刚曼荼罗

The Mandala of Kalacakra Vajra

时轮金刚曼荼罗

The Mandala of Kalacakra Vajra

在藏密的本尊像中，时轮金刚有唐卡画像、金属造像、药泥塑像和墙壁画像等几种，色彩艳丽，画工精细。

时轮金刚曼荼罗有绘画（唐卡、壁画）、平面彩沙画、立体建造等。根据经典记载，绘画曼荼罗的颜料非常讲究，常用的有五种。就连绘画用的笔也是由特殊材料做的，一

middle Brahman line to every direction. The length of each line shall be in compliance with the rules. The forty-eight inner lines are the mandala of mind, from which there extends one hundred and ninety-two lines, which shape the world of big mandala. The mandala outside of that of mind is the mouth mandala and the mandala outside of that of mouth is the body mandala. Usually, the three-dimensional Kalacakra Mandala has four doors: the eastern door, the western door, the southern door and the northern door.

时轮金刚曼荼罗

The Mandala of Kalacakra Vajra

般有紫檀柏木笔、白檀香木笔、人骨笔、乌鸦尾翎翎根笔、金笔、降香木笔、吉祥果树笔等。

修建立体时轮金刚曼荼罗时，首先选择地址，其次打线，阿阇黎坐西面东，左手拿线，左腿半跏趺，右腿置地。弟子在阿阇黎的对面，右手持线，右腿半跏趺，左腿置地。曼荼罗的形状为正方形，在其正中间打第一条梵线。然后，阿阇黎坐南向北，被称为羯摩金刚的弟子面向南，打第二条梵线和风火线、角线等。接下来从南向西、从北向东、从东向南、从西向北打线，从中央的梵线向东、南、西、北打九十六条线，每一条线都有规定的长度。四十八条内线的中央是意曼荼罗，从意曼荼罗向外有一百九十二条线，为大曼荼罗门界。意曼荼罗外有语曼荼罗，语曼荼罗外有身曼荼罗。常见的时轮立体曼荼罗的底层为身曼荼罗，设东西南北四门，内部为语曼荼罗，中心平台上是意曼荼罗，有无上智慧和极乐两部，上面是巨型莲台，时轮金刚与佛

The base is body mandala, in which there is the mouth mandala. The mind mandala is in the center. The mind mandala consists of two parts: the Supreme Wisdom and the Utmost Joy. Above them there is a great lotus seat on which Kalacakra Vajra and Empty and Bliss Mahamudra Buddhamatri sit. Besides them, there are other characters, such as Dakinis, Vajra Bodhisattvas,

时轮金刚曼荼罗

The Mandala of Kalacakra Vajra

时轮金刚曼荼罗

The Mandala of Kalacakra Vajra

母在上面。在整个时轮金刚曼荼罗中除了时轮金刚本尊和空乐佛母外，还有其他空行母、金刚菩萨、传承上师、开派祖师等像。按照经典记载共有722位本尊，分别代表外相的行星和内相的气、脉、明点。

lineage masters and founder masters etc. According to documents, in Kalacakra Mandala there are seven hundred and twenty-two Satyadevatas representing stars, qi, meridians and bindus.

三 胜乐金刚

Cakrasamvara

胜乐金刚

Cakrasamvara

胜乐金刚，亦称“上乐金刚”“大乐金刚”，梵文为Cakrasamvara，藏文为BDe-mCHog。他是藏传佛教无上瑜伽部五大本尊之一，又是胜乐法门的名称。《空行母网律仪》这样描述胜乐金刚的产生：在很早以前的某一时期，世间一片混乱，一切有情表现得极其凶狂暴戾，死后复生为邪恶堕落者。此时瘟疫蔓延，恶魔横行，毁坏三界，修行者被吞噬，诸天神遭诛杀，经论学说毁灭殆尽。为了寻求庇护，诸天神与因陀罗一起，来到梵天前。梵天又与诸神和因陀罗一起，前往毗湿奴处。梵天、毗湿奴和诸神又来到大自在天（湿婆）面前。尔后，梵天、毗湿奴和大自在天于持金刚处求得庇佑。持金刚或大金刚持聚合起一切诸佛，同仇敌忾，决心制伏邪恶堕落者。鉴于那些凶狂暴戾之徒不能通过和平手段降伏，本尊皆以凶恶面目示现。于是，通过调息、与明妃和合等瑜伽术，胜乐金刚诞生了。但见他手持金刚杵，头戴骷髅冠，面目狰狞，形象可怖，如烈火般熊熊燃烧。他的外表为了一切有情而燃为蓝色，他的曼荼罗红光闪烁。他恐怖犹似尸林，凶猛如大毁灭神。他在烈火中凝视与舞蹈，将三界与楼陀罗、大自在天、毗湿奴、日、月、阎摩、梵天以及众魔悉数燃为灰烬，嗣后他们又都重生。而经燃烧的荼吉尼曼荼罗，通过金刚欲与

Cakrasamvara, BDe-mCHog in Tibetan, is one of the five great Satyadevatas and the name of the Dharma of Samvara. *The Rules and Ceremonies of Dakini' s Net* talks about the origin of Cakrasamvara, Once upon a time, the world is in a chaotic mess. All the living beings were extreme rude and brutal, generation by generation. Meanwhile, the plagues spread everywhere and demons were on a rampage, destroying Three Realms. Yogis were devoured and all devas were almost slaughtered. The sutras and treatises were ruined and burned out. As a result, devas, Indra, Brahmadeva, Shiva and Vishnu got together to ask Vajradhara for protection. They joined other Buddhas and use their mind to subdue those demons. Because the demons were very evil, it is impossible to subdue them by peace. Buddha transformed himself into a fierce and malicious appearance and used yoga, such as practicing pranayama and making love with his Buddhamatri, then Cakrasamvara was born. It was said that Cakrasamvara wore a skull crown and take a vajra in his hand. He had a fearful and ferocious face like one in burning fire. His appearance was fired into blue for all living beings and his mandala was shining red. He stared and danced with fire to burn the three worlds and Indra, Mahadeva, Vishnu, Sun and Moon, Yama, Brahmadeva and all demons down. Then they were reborn from ash. Carasamvara cleaned the world and made it peaceful and quiet through burning Dakini Mandala and practicing supreme behaviors, such as vajra desire and fierce.

Cakrasamvara has the ability to use every phantasm. When described as human, he appears as a donkey. There is another saying that at first, Buddha lived in Akanishtha, the highest layer of the Eighting Loka of Rupadhatu, and delivered the Dharma of Samvara on and on until he made himself a manifestation on the top of Sumeru Mount. Later, Buddha lived in Jambudvipa and

凶恶等无上的行为模式，胜乐金刚净化了原本充斥着暴戾、邪恶、有情的各个宇宙，使之变得清净。（参见李南：《〈胜乐根本续〉及其注疏研究》，载《南亚研究》2011 年第 4 期，第 131~145 页）

胜乐金刚具有运用一切幻象的能力，当他被描绘成人的形象时是一副驴形。又说最初佛居住在色界十八天之最高天，即色究竟天，不停地讲胜乐金刚法，直到化现在须弥山顶。后来，佛住南瞻部洲示现十二化机（指释迦牟尼佛示现一生经历的十二件大事，又称十二宏化或十二相成道，即兜率降世、入住母胎、圆满诞生、少年嬉戏、受用妃眷、从家出家、行苦难行、趋金刚座、调伏魔军、成正等觉、转妙法轮、入大涅槃），转三乘法轮；在南印度驮那羯傑迦山（吉祥聚米山）修胜乐三摩地，变化出曼荼罗，为八十万瑜伽母讲胜乐法。为了镇压印度教三大主神之一的湿婆神，佛化现成为六十二胜乐本尊忿怒相，因此称为母续王，被尊为亿万空行者的主人。

湿婆原是古婆罗门教的神，由《吠陀经》所说的楼陀罗神发展而来，有毁灭之神、苦行之神、舞蹈之神的称呼。根据《吠陀经》记载，一般湿婆神的形象被描绘成五头、

showed his twelve moments of life (which refer to the twelve events that Buddha experienced–borning form Tushita, entering in his mother's womb, borning perfectly, playing in early youth, having wives, leaving home and becoming a monk, practicing asceticism, making vajra throne, subduing demons, gaining Samyak Sambodhi, turning the wheel of dharma and nirvana) , and turning the wheel of Triyana. In the Mountain of Dhanakataka in southern India, Buddha practiced the Samvara Samadhi and conjured a mandala for delivering the dharma of Samvara to eight hundred thousand yoginis. Because Buddha transformed himself as sixty-two wrathful appearances of Cakrasamvaras for suppressing Shiva, who is one of the India's three great Lords, he was called the King of Mother Tantra and was respected as the master of hundreds of thousands of dakinis.

Shiva used to be the Lord of ancient Brahmanism and was formerly the Lord of Rudra. According to *Veda Sutra*, Shiva has the name of the Lord of Damage, the Lord of Dushkara charya and the Lord of Dancing. In *Veda Sutra*, it is said, normally, Shiva is painted as having five heads, three eyes, four arms and wearing a fur clothes with his body covered with ash. His four hands hold the trident, divine trumpet shell, water pot and drum respectively. Sometimes, Shiva is carved as having three heads, four faces, ten arms and riding on a white bull, holding weapons, such as a divine spear, a divine bow, a battle-axe or a vajra. When he appeared as the Lord of damage, he wears a skull necklace and looks fierce and ferocious and is easy to be wrathful. When he is the Lord of Dushkaracharya, he is naked and makes hair a plate on his head. Usually, he has four heads with three eyes and every forehead is drawn with a crescent. When he is the Lord of dancing, he continuously performs the dance of destroying the cosmos. When

三目、四臂，手中分别拿着三股叉、神螺、水罐、神鼓，穿着皮衣，全身涂灰。有时也雕成三头、四面、十臂，手执神枪、神弓、战斧、金刚杵等各种兵器，胯下一头白牛。当其显现毁灭之神像时，面目狰狞，性格狂暴，颈挂骷髅项链；显现苦行之神像时，赤身裸体，三眼四头，头盘发辫，额绘弯月；显现舞王之神相时，狂跳可怕的毁灭宇宙之舞；显现再生之神像时，以男根（林伽）代表其形象。（参见尚会鹏：《印度文化史》，广西师范大学出版社2007年版，第142页）又因为胜乐金刚被看成是过去、现在、未来三世诸佛的身、语、意之所依，一切佛功德的总集代表，故称“总摄轮”，别称“空行自在”“金刚轮”“英勇金刚”“月冠冕”“有福”等。

胜乐金刚，是无上瑜伽部母续类法之一，关于此法有种种传说。相传，佛教四劫时（圆满劫时、三分劫时、二分劫时、净劫时）之净劫时开始时，众生相互残杀，把尸体送往八方，形成了八大尸林或八大寒林，即八个弃尸的地方：东方暴虐寒林、北方密丛寒林、南方骨锁寒林、西方金刚焰寒林、东北方狂笑寒林、东南方吉祥寒林、西南方幽暗寒林、西北方啾啾寒林，尸林之气形成八大云，降雨形成八大水，水中生长八种树，出现八条龙，树中出

he appears as the Lord of Rebirth, his image is a penis. Because Cakrasamvara is also regarded as the past, present and future Buddha's support of the body, language and mind and as the symbol of all merits and virtues, he is called Total Holding Wheel, or Dakini Freedom, Vajra Wheel, Brave Vajra, Moon Crown and Possessing Bliss, etc.

There are lots of legends about Cakrasamvara, one of the Mother Tantras of Anuttarayoga. It is said that in the beginning of the Quarrel Kalpa Era Time, the last one of the Four Kalpa Era Times and the other three are Perfect Kalpa Era Time, Trisection Kalpa Era Time and Bisection Kalpa Era Time, all living beings were killing each other and transported the dead bodies to everywhere. Gradually, the gathering areas became the Eight Big Cemeteries (also the Eastern Brutal Cemetery, namely, the Northern Jungle Cemetery, the Southern Bone Cemetery, the Western Vajra Fire Cemetery, the North-eastern Laughing Cemetery, the South-eastern Lucky Cemetery, the South-western Gloomy Cemetery and the North-western Twittering Cemetery). The air in the Eight Big Cemeteries formed eight enormous clouds and the rainfall produced the eight great rivers. Eight kinds of trees were growing and eight dragons appeared in the rivers. Eight divine protectors emerged on those trees. Meanwhile, Mahesvara came by Ubiquitous supernatural power to Sumeru and Jambudvipa, and transformed twenty-four Vajrabhairavas to protect twenty-four places.

Because Mahesvara was transformed from Vajrapani and the Satyadevata of Vajrapani is Cakrasamvara, twenty-four places became the main places for Cakrasamvara to do yoga and spread dharma. Another saying is that in the Quarrel Kalpa , the world was

胜乐金刚

Cakrasamvara

现八方保护神。这时，大自在天利用神通来到须弥山和南瞻部洲，变化出二十四位大威德金刚守护二十四个地方（二十四圣地）。

因为大自在天是由金刚手所变，金刚手的本尊即是胜乐金刚，所以二十四圣地成了胜乐金刚修行传法的主要场所。又说净劫时，世界被大自在天所控制，他的曼荼罗等在许多地方都有显现，其中最主要的就是二十四圣地。当时人们都以杀牲来祭祀大自在天，祈祷得到救护，这种情况令五部勇父空行无法忍受，于是请佛陀传授能降伏镇压大自在天的教法。佛陀便化现出胜乐金刚形象，讲授胜乐金刚法，调伏了大自在天，并将其二十四圣地加持转化为胜乐曼荼罗的二十四圣地，这也是世尊传授灌顶后唯一没有收回，而留在人世间的曼荼罗。根据胜乐经典，这二十四圣地是布拉罗摩罗衍、阇兰达罗、欧乞耶那、阿罗布陀、侨达婆梨、罗摩婆罗、提毗瞿陀罗、摩罗跋、迦摩缕波、兰毗迦、迦尼阇、喜玛拉雅、札达、阇诃提婆、苏洛奢陀罗、须跋罗纳提婆、那迦罗、信度、莫若、格鲁达、遮兰达罗、欧底、多黎沙拘乃、侨萨罗。

胜乐金刚的法相身形有七十二种，常见的有一头二臂、一头四臂和四面十二臂、单腿舞立等。此外，还有最胜上乐金刚（白胜乐金刚）、勇士胜乐金刚、大鹏胜乐金刚（嘎噜底胜乐金刚）、独雄胜乐金刚和本生胜乐金刚等。

controlled by Mahesvara. Mahesvara has mandalas everywhere, but the main ones are twenty-four mandalas in twenty-four places. In that time, people worshiped Mahesvara by killing animals to pray for protection against harm. The Brave Father and Dakinis of Five Family could not endure such situation, so they asked Buddha to suppress Mahesvara. Buddha accepted and transformed himself as Cakrasamvara. He made a speech of the dharma of Cakrasamvara and tamed Mahesvara. He also changed Mahesvara's twenty-four famous spots into twenty-four Cakrasamvara mandalas, this is the first time that after accepting abhisheka Buddha left mandalas in the secular world. According to the sutras of Cakrasamvara, those twenty-four famous spots are pulliramalaya, Dzalan-thara, Otiyana, Arputa, Gotawari, Ramashwar, Devikotra, Malawa, Kamarupa, Lampka, Kanytsi, Himalaya, Pretapur , Grihadeba, Sorashatra, Suwarnadepa, Nagara, Sinthu, Maro, Kuluta and Dzalanthara, etc.

Cakrasamvara has seventy-two dharma bodies. Normally, he has one head and two arms, one head and four arms four faces and twelve arms or standing on one leg in a pose of dancing. Besides, there are Supreme Pravaracakra samvara, Viracakra samvara, Garudacakra samvara and Jatakacakra samvara, etc.

The image with one face and two arms is Sahajacakra samvara. His upper part of his body is ultramarine. He is wearing five-skull crown ornamented by mani jewels, jewelry necklace linked by the beads of fifty skulls and earrings and bangles. The lower part of his body is grey blue and wears tiger fur skirt. He hugged red Vajravarahi with two arms. His left hand takes a Vajra Bell, the other holds a Vajra. He steps on the forehead of Mahesvara with his left leg and his right leg is standing straight on the chest of Mahesvaradevakanya. The Dharanibharya Vajravarahi has one face with three eyes and two arms. Half of her long hair is made into a plate and half loose. She is naked and wears five-skull crown and skull-made necklace. Her left hand holds a skull filled with blood and right hand takes a vajra knife. Her right

胜乐金刚

Cakrasamvara

胜乐金刚

Cakrasamvara

一面二臂是俱生胜乐金刚像，上身青蓝色，头戴五骷髅冠，顶髻有摩尼宝珠，半月相饰。下身灰蓝色，系着虎皮裙。两臂拥抱红色金刚亥母，左右两手分别拿金刚铃和金刚杵，胸前佩挂着用五十颗人头串成的璎珞项链。双耳挂着耳环，手腕套着镯子。左腿微屈，脚踩蓝色大自在天额头。右腿侧直，脚踩红色大自在天女胸口。明妃金刚亥母一面二臂三目，头发半髻半披，全身赤裸，头戴五骷髅冠，项挂五十颗人头项链，左手捧着盛满鲜血的头盖骨，右手持金刚钺刀，右腿勾在胜乐金刚腰间，左腿与胜乐本尊平行站立。

本尊与金刚亥母站在莲花台燃烧的光明智慧光中，三目圆睁，散发光芒，现忿怒相。佛父胜乐金刚的蓝色身，代表“气”，象征慈悲；佛母金刚亥母的红色身，代表“血”，象征智慧，双方相互拥抱，代表气血相依。

在胜乐金刚造像中，最常见的是四面十二臂像，它代表佛位七支金刚身。四头四面，代表佛教的慈无量心、悲无量心、喜无量心和舍无量心。四面的颜色不同，呈威严忿怒相，本面或中面是蓝色，左面白色，右面红色，后面黄色，分别代表增益、息灾、敬爱、降伏四业或红脸代表

leg hugs Cakrasamvara's waist and her left leg stands alongside Cakrasamvara.

The two, Cakrasamvara and Vajravarahi, stand in the shining wisdom on lotus seat. They open their three eyes widely and brightly to show their angry. The blue of Cakrasamvara represents qi, symbolizing mercy. The red of Vajravarahi represents blood, signifying wisdom. Their embrace symbolizes the inter-dependence of qi and blood.

The most common statues of Cakrasamvara are those with four faces and twelve arms which represent the diamond body of seven branches state of Buddhahood. The four faces are the symbols of boundless kindness, boundless compassion, boundless joy and limitless impartiality. Different face has different color and meaning. The front face is blue, symbolizing increasing; the left is yellow, symbolizing the ceasing misfortune; the right is green, symbolizing respecting and loving; the back one is black, symbolizing taming. Or the red face symbolizes respexcting and loving, the green face symbolizes ceasing misfortune, the black face symbolizes taming, and the yellow face symbolizes increasing. Every face has three eyes, one of them on the forehead, looking upward, the other two open widely. They observe the past, the present and the future intuitively. His ears extend to the shoulders and wear big earrings. The Buddha crown he wears is decorated with five skulls, which stands for the five Buddhas from five directions, representing all impermanence and courage. On the top of his hair, there are a crescent which is the symbol of happiness of all living beings, and double vajras representing method and wisdom. A necklace with fifty skull beads is hanging on his chest, which means all

胜乐金刚

Cakrasamvara

敬爱、绿脸代表息灾、黑脸代表降伏、黄脸代表增益。每一面有三只眼，其中额头上一眼向上看，其余二目圆睁，表示能够观照过去、现在、未来三世。他双耳垂肩，佩戴大耳环；头戴着由五骷髅装饰的佛冠，代表五方佛，象征一切无常和勇敢；上方有半月形，代表众生的幸福；顶有

sutras of Buddha. A tiger fur is tied around his waist, symbolizing fearlessness and courage. His twelve blue arms are the symbol of overcoming the Twelve Dependent Origination, such as ignorance, action, consciousness, name and form, the six senses, contact, feeling, thirst, grasp, becoming, born, aging and death. He uses his main pair of arms to hug Dharanibharya Vajravarahi with a vajra in the right hand and a vajra bell in the left hand. The rest ten hands

胜乐金刚

Cakrasamvara

双金刚，表示方便与智慧双运；项挂用五十颗人头串成的项链，代表佛所有的经典；腰间围系带有虎尾的虎皮，表示无畏和勇猛；十二手臂全是蓝色，象征克服无明、行、识、名色、六处、触、受、爱、取、有、生、老死十二缘起的方法，左右主臂拥抱明妃金刚亥母，左手拿金刚铃、右手持金刚杵，其余十手做出不同的样子，分别拿着人头、如意宝绳、头盖骨、战斧、月形刀、三叉戟、骷髅杖、金刚绳、金刚钩等；左腿微屈，呈弓步，脚踩仰卧的时间女神（黑夜叉女），代表调伏嗔恨，右腿侧直，脚踩一俯身半裸的大自在天（怖畏湿婆），代表超越世间。

又说胜乐金刚有红、绿、黑、黄四面，每一面有三目，表示能观照过去、现在和未来三世，照顾一切有情。两条腿代表方便与智慧，右腿伸开，表示传播教法，脚下踩着怖畏湿婆神，表示降伏了忿怒；左腿弯曲，表示快乐已被接受，脚踩黑夜叉女，表示降伏了色欲。他背后披白象皮，腰间围虎皮裙，象征勇猛无畏。胜乐金刚拥抱着的红色的明妃金刚亥母右手上扬，挥舞着钺刀，以便杀死一切恶者，并铉住一切善者；以骷髅头念珠做装饰，象征通过布施、持戒、忍辱、精进、禅定和智慧六种方法，从生死此岸到达涅槃彼岸，获得解脱。

hold different things, such as people's head, a rope made by mani jewel, a skull, a battle ax, a half moon-like knife, a trident, a skull cane, a vajra rope and a vajra hook etc. His left leg bends a little and steps on Krsnayaksnini, who is the deity wasting time. This means subduing anger. His right leg keeps straight and tramples on half-naked Bhairavamshiva, which means surpassing this world.

It is also said that Cakrasamvara has four faces which are red, green, black and yellow, each having three eyes. Cakrasamvara uses the three eyes to observe the past, the present and the future intuitively and to take care all living beings. His two legs are for method and wisdom. The right leg is outstretching and represent the spreading of Buddhism, Bhairavamshiva under his right foot means his taming angry. The left leg bents slightly that shows he accepts happiness. Krsnayaksnin under his left foot means he tames sexual desire. He wears white elephant fur, a tiger fur around his waist representing brave and fearlessness. The red Dharanibharya Vajravarahi is held by him takes a half moon-like knife in the right hand to kill all evils and maintain all good. Her skull necklace is the symbol of the six methods of nirvana, namely: almsgiving, keeping commandments, patience under insult, pure progress, meditation and wisdom, all these help practitioners to go to the other shore.

When Tucci, the famous Italian Tibetologist, searched the Temple of TSa-Pa-Rang, he found a statue of Cakrasamvara in Samvara Hall. He described that the Lucky Heruka（Another name of Cakrasamvara）was blue and sitting in the center of the lotus throne. The main face of the four faces was black, the left one green, the back one red and the right one yellow. Every face had three eyes. He had twelve arms, the main pair of arms crossed in

意大利著名藏学家图齐在二十世纪三十年代考察西藏阿里地区的扎布让寺时，发现胜乐殿有胜乐金刚像，他描述道："中央莲心日座上为世尊吉祥呬噜嘎，身蓝色；四面之主面黑，左面绿，背面红，右面黄，各面具三眼；十二臂；额佩五股金刚杵鬘；右足伸展，压于双手合十、余右手执瓕鼓、左手执剑之四臂怖畏黑天之首；左足弯曲，压于双手合十、余二手持颅器及天杖之红色四臂迦利之乳。……（呬噜嘎）双手环抱金刚亥母，右手持五股金刚杵，左手持铃；此下之双手在身后伸展一带血之白色象皮衣，右手执左前肢，左手执左后肢，施期克印之两手指尖与眉齐平；右第三手举瓕鼓、第四手举钺斧、第五手举钺刀、第六手举三叉戟；左第三手持有金刚标志（菩提心之自性）之天杖、第四手持盛满鲜血（大乐味之自性）之颅器、第五手持金刚羂索、第六手持四面梵头，梵头具有交杵金刚标志之辫髻；各首有黑金刚鬘，其上下饰有五人头骷髅贯穿之鬘，悬有稍向头左侧歪斜之半月；面具具种种变，每面四獠牙突出，甚堪怖畏；具九种姿态：娇媚、豪迈、可厌三身姿态，豪野、暴戾、堪怖三语姿态，恻隐、威猛、平和三意姿态；系虎皮裙；（从颈至大腿处）悬挂有穿于人肠上之五十颗湿人头鬘；以六印为标记；以人骨

front of the chest, the rest right arms holding drums and left arms taking swords. He straightened the right foot and bent the left foot... Heruka hugged Vajravarahi with a vajra in the right hand and a vajra bell in the left hand. The two hands of the next are stretching the bloody white elephant leather at behind area, right hand holding the left forefoot makes a Tarjani Gesture and trying to get two fingers as the same level as eyebrow; left hand is holding the left hindleg. The right third hand holds a drum, the fourth hand holds an axe, the fifth hand holds a knife, the sixth hand holds a trident; the third hand of the left holds a cane, fourth hand holds a cranial in full with blood, fifth hand holds a belt of cable, the sixth hand holds a four-face Brahman's head, which hair worn in a bun like Vajra cross around; each head has black beautiful hairs and linked with five skeletons, hanging on a half-moon shape of ornaments with a bit skew to the left of head. His masks can show different kinds, each face has four prominent tusks, all of images look terrible. He has namby-pamby, bold and disgusting three body-postures; wild, violent and terrible three karmas; compassion, brave and calm active minds nine postures in all. He wears tiger-skin skirt, (from the neck to his thigh) hanging fifty wet heads on intestines; with the tag of the six seals. Ashes of people spread on the whole body.

Dharanibharya Vajravarahi has one face, two arms and a red body, symbolizing the passionate love as well as blood and compassion. She looks up, wearing a skull crown and a skull necklace. Her right hand takes a crescent knife while her left hand holds a skull filled with blood. Her two legs hug Cakrasamvara's waist. Tucci said that Buddhamatri Vajravarahi faced Cakrasamvara. She was red and had one face with three eyes, two arms and long hair. She wore a skull-made waist chain. Her left arm embraced Cakrasamvara. Her left hand held a skull containing four demons' blood to feed

胜乐金刚

Cakrasamvara

灰涂抹全身。”（[意]图齐著，魏正中、萨尔吉主编：《梵天佛地》第三卷《西藏西部的寺院及其艺术象征》第二册，上海古籍出版社 2009 年版，第 11~12 页）

明妃金刚亥母一面二臂，身呈红色，既表示爱慕热烈，又代表悲心和“血”。他面朝上仰望，头戴骷髅冠，颈戴人头项链，右手拿弯月刀，左手拿盛满鲜血的头盖骨，双腿紧勾胜乐金刚腰部或左腿微屈，右腿曲盘于胜乐金刚腰间。图齐说：“薄伽梵母金刚亥母面对世尊，身红色；一面二臂；三眼；赤体披发；具头骨骷髅片为饰之腰带垂穗；勾父颈之左手持盛满四魔等鲜血之颅器，并呈之父口；右手持金刚，并以期克印对十方一切凶暴者施以威吓。”

米旁南杰在他的《时轮根本续·智慧品释》中写道：“在莲花中心的太阳上面有胜乐本尊，左腿微屈，右腿伸直，脚踩邬摩天女和大自在天。他身呈蓝黑色，如同灭劫之云，头上戴着五骷髅冠。胜乐金刚本面黑色，右面红色，左面白色，后面黄色。具有压服十二缘起的十二手的呬噜嘎，围着饰有六手印和十条蛇的虎皮裙；主二臂拥抱绿色佛母金刚亥母，手中分别拿着钺刀和头盖骨碗。在大乐轮之外，有黑色意轮、红色语轮和净如月亮的身轮……”这是米旁

Cakrasamvara, while her right hand took a vajra to threaten all demons.

Jamgon Mipham writes in *the Commentary of Wisdom of Kalacakra Mulagrantha Tantra* that Samvara Satyadevata is in the center of lotus. He bends his right leg a little, straightens the left leg and steps on Deviuma and Mahesvara Ishvaradeca. His body is black-blue, much like dark clouds. He wears a five-skull crown. His own face is black, while other transformed faces are red, white and yellow respectively. The Heruka with twelve hands can force the Twelve Dependent Origination under his will, who wears piece of tiger-skin skirt that ornaments six mudra gestures and ten snake-paintings. His main arms hug green skin Dharanibharya Vajravarahi with a tomahawk knife and skull bowl in two hands respectively, outside the Big Happiness Wheel, there are Black Mind Wheel, Red Language Wheel and Moon-like Color Body Wheel. Jamgon Mipham's depiction of the image Samvara Satyadevata in mandala likes this: he is surrounded by a lot of wrathful Buddhamatris, Deviuma and other female deities, and each of them holds a dharma instrument.

According Buddhist classicals that in general there are fourteen different dharmas instrument held or worn by Cakrasamvara that is six ornaments made bone (including Buddha's crown decorated by five skulls, eardrops, necklace made by human's heads, tassels made by human's bones, borne-made hand bracelets, borne-made foot bracelets), rouge made by human's fat, daubing ash, paint-liquid made by human blood, skull, heaven rod, machete, drum, tambourine, trombope, human corpse mat, tiger skin mat, human skin coat, tiger skin apron. In Qing Dynasty, the tradition of DGe

南杰所描绘的曼荼罗中的胜乐本尊的形象，其周围有许多忿怒佛母、邬摩天女和其他女神，各个手持法器。

佛教典籍说，一般胜乐金刚本尊穿着的服饰和手中的法器有十四种：骨质六庄严（五骷髅佛冠、耳坠、人头项链、骨瓔珞、骨手钏、骨足镯）及人脂胭脂、涂灰、人血涂液、头盖骨、天杖、弯刀、簸鼓、小鼓、长号、人尸垫、虎皮垫、人皮衣、虎皮围裙。清代画的格鲁派传承的胜乐金刚像以四首十二臂为多，头戴五骷髅冠，腰系虎皮裙，身披象皮披风，项挂人头项链，足踩两个魔鬼，主臂抱金刚亥母。画面背光为火焰，四角有四位空行母，呈现红、黄、蓝、绿四色。不过，胜乐金刚也有其他不同的形象。

胜乐法门的根本经典《胜乐根本续》共五十一品，七百颂，内容涉及多种多样的复杂设置和如何迎请各方本尊，各种灌顶法、真言咒语和手印仪轨，生起次第和圆满次第的修行法，身曼荼罗的多种修炼法，对本尊神胜乐金刚、金刚亥母、诸瑜伽母、三十七位空行者的观想供养方法，对二十四圣地的描述，通过标记加持而识别瑜伽母的特殊性相仪轨，弟子所需持守之律仪仪轨，依靠空行母修炼俱生智慧的具体方法，以及有关饮食、护摩的仪轨，等等，

Lugs Pa painted Cakrasamvara with four faces and twelve arms, wearing a Buddha's crown decorated by five skulls, tying with a tiger skin skirt, wearing a elephant skin cloak, hanging a necklace made by human's heads, and steping on two devils, embraceing Vajravarahi with his main arms. The context if the painting is flame, four dakinis on four corners are red, yellow, blue and green respectively. Sometimes, Cakrasamvara appears in other different forms.

Samvara Fundamental Tantra, the main sutra of Samvara Dharma, has fifty-one chapters and including seven hundred verses. It contains kinds of madalas including their setting methods, inviting methods of every Satyadevata, empowering methods, holding the rites of mandras and mudra gestures. It also has the method of practicing Arising Orderly and Perfecting Orderly and exercising various body-mandalas, and the method of the observation and offerings of Heruka, Vajravarahi, yoginis and thirty-seven dakinis. This sutra depicts twenty-four holy places and recognizes yoginis by marking special rites. It tells disciples how to guard moral laws'rites, and how to practice inborn intelligence by depending on dakinis. There are still some rites about food and homa, ete, and some special Yogini Tantra methods of practicing qi, meridians, wheels, bindus, fierce fire and bodhi mind and so on.

Cakrasamvara Mandala is complicated and has rigorous rules. Its lines, materials and arrangements all follow strict principles. Commonly, a Samaya Mandala is a cubit long; a Siddhi Mandala's four sides are a cubit long; an Abhisheke Mandala is four to eight cubit long, sometimes four to twenty cubits. The five painting materials are of different qualities: high quality, medium quality

胜乐金刚曼荼罗

The Mandala of Cakrasamvara

胜乐金刚曼荼罗
The Mandala of Cakrasamvara

还讲述了气、脉、轮、明点、猛厉火和菩提心等瑜伽母续所特有的修炼法。

胜乐金刚曼荼罗设计比较复杂，每一步都有非常严格的规定，如画线、使用颜料、安置本尊等。一般规定的标准是三昧耶曼荼罗的尺寸为一肘（相当于二十四指宽），修行悉地的曼荼罗每面各一肘，授灌顶的曼荼罗为四到八肘，也有四肘至二十肘的。五种颜料分劣质、中等、优质三类，其中劣质颜料五种全出自寒林（尸林），即蓝色是由尸灰和木灰调制成的，红色是用骨灰和火砖调制成的，白色是用骨灰和阳起石粉调成的，黄色是用

and poor quality. The poor one comes from the Cemetery. The blue painting material is made of the ash of corpses and woods; the red is made of the ash of bones and firebricks; the white is by bone ashes and stone powder; the yellow is by bone ashes and arsenolite powder or curcuma powder; the green is by bone ashes and the leave juice. The medium one is made of grains. The high-quality material is made of five gemstones.

Cakrasamvara Mandala consists of the outer city and the inner city. The outer city includes four circles: Vajra Circle, Eight Big Cemeteries Circle, Lotuses Circle and the gates. The inner city comprises of five circles, including Samaya Circle, Mystic Body Circle, Mystic Language Circle, Mystic Mind Circle and Mahasukha Circle. In the Mandala, there are sixty-two Satyadevatas. Each of Mystic Body Circle, Mystic Language Circle and Mystic Mind Circle has eight gates, totaling twenty-four objects.

胜乐金刚曼荼罗

The Mandala of Cakrasamvara

骨灰和砒石或姜黄粉调成的，绿色是用骨灰和尸林中的树叶汁调成的。中等颜料是用谷物调成的，优质颜料是用五种珠宝调成的。

胜乐金刚曼荼罗的结构是：墙外第一层为金刚圈，代表金刚火焰；第二层为八大寒林；第三层为莲花层，表示慈悲心；第四层为城门。墙内有五重同心圆或五圈，由外到内依次是三昧耶轮、身密轮（身成就）、语密轮、意密轮、大乐轮，共有六十二位本尊。身、语、意各有八门，共二十四门，代表二十四境。大乐轮中央是本尊胜乐金刚。《胜乐根本续》解释说：曼荼罗以吉祥胜乐金刚和金刚亥母为中心神，他们被四位核心瑜伽母荼吉尼、上师母、碎生母和有形母所拱卫。这六位神明共同构成了曼荼罗中央的智慧轮。三个同轴之轮环绕着他们，分别是蓝色的意轮、红色的语轮和白色的身轮。每一轮由八对神明组成。曼荼罗周围由八位怖畏女神护卫，分列于八个方位。这些组成了曼荼罗，并被“八大尸林”环绕。

胜乐法传承大师鲁耶巴说，胜乐本尊威严可怖，面色如雨层云，全身布满灭火之光，嘴中不停地发出“哈哈”声，狂笑不止；头戴骷髅冠，四面各有三只眼，身披大象

Cakrasamvara is in the middle of Mahasukha Circle. According to *the Kalacakra Fundamental Tantra*, Heruka and Vajravarahi are the key deities of Cakrasamvara Mandala, surrounded by four kernel Yoginis: Vajrayogini, the Deities of Guru's Wives, Smashed Born Female Deity and Visible Female Deity, who, together, constitute Wisdom Circle. Similarly, the blue Mystic Mind Circle, the red Mystic Language Circle and the white Mystic Body Circle are all surrounded by eight deities. There are still eight fearful female deities outside the inner city for as protectors.

皮，主臂二手分别持金刚铃和金刚杵，其余手各持法器；眉毛竖起，怒目而视。意密轮有八瓣莲，表示明点和观空成就，四角各放一只宝瓶，四方有空行母、各大传承上师等像。语、身、三昧耶三轮分别是蓝色、红色、白色，每一轮各有八尊呈双身像的勇父与空行母。

Lu-Hi-Pa, a guru of Samvara Dharma, said that the Satyadevata of Samvara was very majestic and fearful. His face was like nimbostratus, while his body was full of the light of disaster. He was laughing without stop. The Mystic Mind Circle's eight petals lotus mean bindus and the achievement of empty watching with mental insight. Four treasure vases were put on the four corners of the Mandala. Images of dakinis and lineage gurus were placed in the four directions.

胜乐金刚曼荼罗

The Mandala of Cakrasamvara

四 喜金刚

Hevajra

喜金刚
Hevajra

喜金刚，又称“呼金刚”“欢喜金刚”“饮血金刚”等，梵文为 Hevajra，藏文为 DPal-Kye-rDo-rJe 或 DGav-Ba' i-rDo-rJe，译意为吉祥喜金刚。“He”意为大悲性，“vajra”是智慧的意思，故喜金刚又译“大悲空智金刚”。喜金刚是藏传佛教无上瑜伽部五大本尊之一，萨迦派的主供本尊。关于喜金刚，传说他是大自在天湿婆神的长子。湿婆是婆罗门教和印度教的三大主神（梵天、毗湿奴、湿婆）之一，是由《吠陀经》所说的楼陀罗神发展而来的，具有极大的降魔能力，额上第三只眼的神火能烧毁一切，曾把妖魔的三座城域和爱神烧成灰烬，是宇宙毁灭力量的象征。“他手持强弓，身缠虎皮，巡游于山野，袭击人畜，天上诸神都惧怕他。”（尚会鹏著:《印度文化史》，广西师范大学出版社 2007 年版，第 101 页）其形象被描绘成五头、三目、四手，手中分别拿着三叉戟、神螺、水罐、法鼓，穿着兽皮，坐骑是一头大白牛，颈缠一条蛇，和妻子明妃迦梨女神在喜马拉耶山中修行。佛教称他为大自在天，住在色界之顶，为三千世界之共主。他的另一位妻子邬摩天女皮肤黝黑，“大张着口，伸出舌头，虫蛇绕身，在死尸上跳舞，耳环是用人的尸体做成的，项链是骷髅，面孔和胸乳涂满鲜血，四只手中的

Hevajra, DPal-Kye-rDo-rJe or DGav-Ba'i-rDo-rJe in Tibetan, is one of the five great Satyadevatas of Supreme Yoga Tantra in Tibetan Buddhism. "He" means great compassion and "vajra" is for wisdom. So Hevajra is also called the Great Compassion with Empty Wisdom Vajra. Sometimes, he is called Happy Vajra, Drinking Blood Vajra. Hevajra is worshiped by the Sakya School as their main satyadevata. Stories said that Hevajra was the first son of Shiva. Shiva, one of three main Hindu deities (including Brahma, Vishinu and Shiva), was developed from Rudra in *Vada Sutra* and possesses huge power to subdue demons. His third eye on the forehead can spout divine fire to destroy everything. Because Shiva once used the third eye to burn down demons' three cities and Kama, the deity of love, his third eye is regarded as the symbol of destroying power. Shang Huipeng said in *Hindu Cultural History* that he who held the powerful bow and wore tiger fur cruised to attack people and animals. All deities were afraid of him. His image is portrayed as five heads, three eyes, four hands. His hands held trident, divine conch, water pot and dharma drum. He wears a coat and rides a big white buffalo. A snake coils around his neck. His wife, Devikali, accompanies him practice dharma in Himalayas. Buddhists call him Mahesvara and think he live in the top of Rupadhatu, is the common lord of Great Triple-thousand worlds. Deviuma, Hevajra's another wife, has dark skin and is dancing on human's corpses. She opens her mouth largely, sticks out her tongue. Worms and snakes around her body. Her earrings are made of human's corpses, necklace made of human's skulls. Blood is painted on her face and chest. She has four hands, two hands hold sword and human's head, two hands make protecting mudra gestures and bless mudra gesture respectively. She is the Death and the Fertility. She is cruel but also gentle, can kill but also smile.

两只执利剑和人头，另两只手则伸开作保护和祝福状。她是死亡之神，又是生育之神，既残忍也温和，既能杀戮也能微笑”。（尚会鹏著：《印度文化史》，广西师范大学出版社 2007 年版，第 173 页）

她生有 3000 个儿子，左右两边各站 1500 个，右边的 1500 个为毗那夜迦王，人身象鼻，经常在世间行施诸恶。左边的 1500 个为扇那夜迦王，是观世音菩萨的化身，以行善积德、调伏恶魔为己任。所以，为了镇服毗那夜迦王，扇那夜迦王变化成为女身，与毗那夜迦王结成“兄弟夫妇”，显现拥抱像。善无畏译的《大圣欢喜供养法》中又说，大自在天的长子欢喜金刚是一个残害世界的大荒之神，观世音菩萨化身为明妃拯救世界，帮助危难者，通过拥抱吸尽丈夫荒神的恶源，镇压摄受邪恶及邪欲，以达到自在欢喜的目的，故称“欢喜天”。

喜金刚是从湿婆神的形象发展演变而来的，《喜金刚根本续》说喜金刚全身为黑色，有十六臂、八面、四足，项挂头骨花环，头顶十字金刚杵，穿戴五种庄严，脚踩四魔，在日轮上狂怒而舞。据文献记载：“我的身上涂着灰，嘴中发出‘吽’字声音。然而我内在的特质是沉静，并与

She has three thousand sons. One thousand and five hundred sons stand on her right side and they are Vinayaka Kings. They have human body and elephant nose. They always do all evil thing in world. One thousand and five hundred sons stand on her left side and are Sannayaka Kings, the transformations of Avalokitesvara. They do good deeds and take charge of taming demons. For the sake of taming Vinayaka Kings they transform themselves as women to merry with Vinayaka Kings, become brother couples and hug each other. *Great Holy Joy Offering Ritual*, written by Subhakarasimha, says that Hevajra, the eldest son of Mahesvara, is a cruel deity who harms and devastate living beings in the world. For saving the world, Avalokitesvara transformed herself as Hevajra's dakini. She embraced him and sucked dry the evils of her husband and suppressed his evil desire. Because of this they attained the aim of being joy, so this be called Ganapati.

Shiva is the former of Hevajra. *Hevajra Fundamental Tantra* said, Hevajra has a black body, sixteen arms, eight faces and four feet, wearing skull garland around his neck. A vajra is on his head. Wearing five kinds of ornaments, he is stepping on four demons and dancing on them. Another saying is that Hevajra paints ash on his body and says 'hom'. But he has inner peace. He hugs and loves dakini Anatman. He is immersing in great happiness. The front face of Hevajra is black, the right face is white like jasmine flower, the left face is red which makes people fear. The back face of him is twisted. Other faces like bees have twenty-four eyes.

It is said in *the Rules and Ceremonies of Hevajra and Dakini's Illusory Net* that Hevajra has eight faces, eight feet and sixteen arms. His eight feet steps on Four Demons (Afflictions Demon, Aggregates Demon, Deva Demon and Death Demon, another

无我母爱恋地相拥抱，我正被沉静大乐所支配。我前面的脸是黑色，右边的脸是茉莉白色，左边的脸是红色，令人可怖，而后面的脸是扭曲变形的，其余的脸就像蜜蜂一样。在那儿共有二十四只眼睛等。"

《喜金刚空行母幻网律仪轨》说："八面有八足，十六只手臂，足踩四妖魔（烦恼魔、蕴魔、天魔、死魔，或黄色大梵天、白色帝释天、蓝色遍入天、黑色大自在天），怖畏又怖畏。头髻作璎珞，住日而乐声，色黑极怖畏，金刚当顶饰；口中发'哄'音，全身满涂灰，无我俱等合，等引四欢喜，顺利得快乐，无慢心本体；本面是黑色，右面为黑色，左红而惧畏，顶饰忿怒相，二十四只眼，其余面黑色。"

常见的喜金刚是双身像，八面、四足、十六臂。八面，象征能够舍弃对色无色的贪欲的八种解脱，即内有色、外观色解脱，内无色、外观色解脱，净色解脱，空无边处解脱，识无边处解脱，无所有处解脱，非想非非想处解脱，灭受想解脱。两面在前，左右各三面，呈寂静和忿怒二相。另一种说法是，八面中三面在前，其中，本面和左面红色，右面白色；后有四面，均为黑色，顶面为青灰色。

saying is yellow Brahmadeva, white Indra, blue Vishnu and black Mahashvara). He is extremely horrible. His hair is made into a topknot decorated with jewelries and vajra. He is saying 'hom'. He uses ash cover his body and make love with Anatmandakini , from which he gets four kinds of joy of Samahita and non-arrogance itself. His main face is black, the right face is black, the left face is red which is wrathful and horrible, other faces are black. He has twenty-four eyes,

Commonly, Hevajra shows his Twin-bodied image, has eight faces, eight feet and sixteen arms. Eight faces mean liberation from eight material and immaterial desires, namely (1) liberating from insight into inner form and observe outer form, (2) liberating from insight into inner formlessness and observe outer form, (3) liberating from pure form, (4) liberating from the base of infinite space, (5) liberating from the base of infinite consciousness, (6) liberating from the base of nothingness, (7) liberating from the base of neither perception nor non-perception, (8) liberating from cessation of perception and feeling. Two of his eight faces are looking forward. And there are three smiling faces on the left and three angry faces on the right. Another saying is that three of the faces are looking forward, the middle face and the left face are red, the right one is white. Four of the face are on the back and all black. The last one face is higher than others, which is also looking forward and grey color. Every face has three eyes which represent the pure and clean of body, language and mind. He wears a skull crown like other Satyadevatas and fifty-skull-made necklace, symbolizing fifty alphabets of Sanskrit. His eight right hands hold skulls in which containers a white elephant, a green horse, a white donkey, a red

每面有三只眼，代表身、语、意三清净。他头戴人骨冠，项挂五十颗骷髅项链，象征梵文五十个字母，八个右手的颅器中分别有白象、绿马、白驴、红狐、灰蛇、红人、绿羚羊、猫神，《喜金刚根本续》说是大象、马、驴、公牛、骆驼、男人、狮子、猫，另外也有说是白象、青鹿、青驴、

fox, a grey snake, a red person, a green gazelle and a divine cat. *Hevajra Fundamental Tantra* thinks the eight things are elephant, horse, donkey, bull, camel, man, lion, cat. There are still another saying thinks the eight things are white elephant, blue deer, blue donkey, red bull, grey camel, red person, blue lion and red cat. His eight left hands hold eight skulls which contain the Yellow Earth Deity, the Clean Water Deity, the Green Wind Deity, the Red Fire Deity, the Red Sun Deity, the White Moon Deity, the Yama (or Green Death Deity) and the Vaishravana (or Yellow Demon), these deities are facing Hevajra. All these sixteen things mentioned above mean sixteen Buddhism Empties, that is inner empty, outer empty, inner and outer empty, emptying the empty, great empty, the highest true empty, conditioned

喜金刚

Hevajra

红牛、灰驼、红人、青狮、赤猫的。他八个左手颅器中有黄土神、白水神、绿风神、红火神、红日神、白月神、阎摩王（绿死神）、多闻天（黄夜叉），各个面向本尊。这十六持物象征佛教十六种空性：内空、外空、内外空、空空、大空、胜义空、有为空、无为空、毕竟空、无际空、无散空、本性空、相空、一切法空、无性空、无所缘空。喜金刚四条腿呈舞蹈姿势，即以半跏趺舞姿立于莲花台座上，里面的左右二腿向内弯曲，外右腿侧直，左腿稍屈，脚踏仰卧之人，象征摄受和降伏邪恶与无明。按照《喜金刚本续》的说法，本尊有代表五方佛的头环、耳环、项链、手镯、腰带，即头环代表不动金刚佛，耳环代表阿弥陀佛，项链代表宝生佛，手镯代表大日如来佛，腰带代表不空成就佛。通过五方佛的修行法，清除贪、嗔、痴、慢、疑五毒。

另外，喜金刚也有四臂像和六臂像，但很少见。四臂喜金刚本尊代表摧伏四魔，他身为蓝黑色或暗蓝色，红色两眼圆睁，黄发竖起，同样有代表五方佛的装饰头环、耳环、项链、手镯、腰带。四臂中一对左右手分别持盛满鲜血的颅器和金刚铃，另外两手拥抱金刚亥母。六臂本尊有三面，前边一面呈蓝黑色，左面红色，右面白色。六臂象征到达六波罗蜜多彼岸，第一对左右手分别持三叉戟与金刚杵，第二对左右手分别拿着金刚铃和钺刀，另两只手拥抱明妃

empty, unconditioned empty, ultimate empty, boundless empty, unmoved empty, self-natural empty, form empty, all dharma empty, selfless empty, non-object empty. Four legs are in a dancing pose on the flat of lotus. Two front legs are stepping on two persons, symbolizing overcoming evil and ignorance. According to *Hevajra Fundamental Tantra*, the five skulls embedded in his crown mean five Buddhas in five directions. And his head-ring means Aksobhyavajra Buddha, his earrings mean Amitabha Buddha, his necklace means Ratnasambhava, his bracelet Vairocana Buddha and his belt Amoghasiddhi. Due to these five Buddhas do practice tantra, the five poisons, that is desire, hatred, stupidity, arrogance and doubt are cleaned away.

Besides, also quite rare, there are also images of Hevajra with four arms or six arms. The four-arm Hevajra, usually with a black blue body, staring eyes and erecting yellow hair, represents beating down the four evils. He uses two arms to hug Vajravarahi and another two hold a skull and a vajra respectively. The six-arm Hevajra has three faces. In which, the middle face is black blue, the left one is red and the right one is white. The six arms are the symbols of Six Paramitas. The first pair of his six hands are holding a trident and a vajra. The second pair of hands are holding a vajra bell and a tomahawk. The last pair of hands hug his Vajrapasha Bodhisattva Dakini . His feet step on a corpse.

The Anatman Dakini who is hugged by one-face and two-arms Hevajra has a black-blue body, red eyes and yellow hair. She has one face and two arms. She wears five-skull crown. Her left arm hugs Hevajra and holds a skull container in the hand, while her right hand holds a knife. Her left foot steps on a man like Hevajra does, while her right leg twine around the waist of Hevajra. *Hevajra Fundamental Tantra* said that the dakini of Anatman is the master of Hevajra Mandala. The nature of her is Dharma, great happiness. The alphabet "A" means wisdom and is the symbol of her nature.

喜金刚曼荼罗

The Mandala of Hevajra

金刚锁菩萨，脚踩一具尸体。

一面二臂喜金刚怀抱的明妃金刚无我佛母，面呈深蓝黑色，两眼发红，头发黄色，头戴五骷髅冠，一面二臂，一手拿钺刀，一手拿颅器，又说右手上扬持曲刀，左腿紧贴本尊右腿侧直立，右腿上扬，威立在莲花座上。本尊喜金刚右腿站立在莲花座上，双脚各踩二仰卧之人，表示降伏邪恶与无明。明妃双腿盘在喜金刚腰间，有时左脚踩着挣扎的男人，右脚踩着挣扎的女人。《喜金刚根本续》说：无我佛母是曼荼罗的主人，本质上是“法”，是檀脑，是大乐。大乐的体悟是“大象征”自身，由阿字（A）表示，阿字象征智慧，即启悟者把金刚无我佛母观想成为智慧。

一般唐卡画和坛城中的喜金刚本尊的周围有许多明妃或空行母，上方正中是贝塔莉空行母，表示五蕴中“想”清净，她身呈黄色，右手拿龟，左手捧颅器，位于西方；上左为军荼莉空行母，她身呈蓝黑色或暗色，代表四大中之火大清净，右手高举法轮，左手在下持犁，位于西南方；上右为东比空行母，身呈黄色，代表风大清净，右手持金

Generally, in Thangka paintings, there are many Dakinis who surround Hevajra. The painting is separated into two parts by Hevajra - the upper part and the lower part. On the upper part of painting, there are three dakinis: Petari Dakini ,Juntari Dakini and Dongbi Dakini. Petari Dakini , the symbol of pure perception which is one of the Five Aggregates, is arranged in the middle and in charge of the west. She is in yellow skin with a turtle in the right hand and a skull container in the left hand. Juntari Dakini is standing on the left and in charge of the south-west. She has a black-blue body and symbolizes the pure and clean fire which is one of the Four Elements. Her right hand holds a dharma wheel highly, while her left hand takes a plough below. Dongbi Dakini is on the right side and in charge of the north-west. She has a yellow body and represents the pure and clean wind of the four elements. Her right hand holds a vajra, while her left hand makes Tarjani gesture. On the lower part of the painting there are five Dakinis, the red Heri Dakini, Kesimarui Dakini, Gori Dakini , Sawarui Dakiniand Bukakasi Dakini. Starting at left, the first one is red Heri Dakini who is in charge of the south. She takes a skull drum in the right hand and a boar in the left hand. She is the symbol of the pure and clean sound. The second one is KesimaruiDakini who is in charge of communicating between the underground world and the upper world. She has a jade-green body, takes a skull bowl in the left hand and a snake in the right hand. She represents the pure and clean taste and nirvana. The third one is the Gori Dakini who is in charge of the east. She is black-skinned and holds a curved knife in the right hand and a fish in the left hand. Gori Dakini means the pure and clean material. The fourth one is white

大清乾隆年敬造

刚杵，左手施期剋印，位于西北方；左侧是红色诃黎空行母，代表声清净，其右手拿着颅鼓，左手抓着野猪，位于南方；右侧是葛斯玛瑞空行母，身翠绿色，代表味清净，表示涅槃，左手捧着颅碗，右手拿着一条蛇，位于地下；下正中是高黎空行母，身黑色，代表色清净，右手持钺刀，左手拿鱼，位于东方；左下为沙瓦瑞空行母，身白色，代表水大清净，右手托着一个比丘僧，左手拿着一把扇子，位于东南方；右下是布嘎嘎斯空行母，身蓝色，代表地大清净，右手捧着一只白狮子，左手高举金刚斧，位于东北。跟喜金刚本尊一样，每位空行母脚下各踩一个人。

为了反映喜金刚的法理，喜金刚本尊有身、语、意三种，分别在地下、天顶和中央。身喜金刚是喜金刚的幻化身，表示一切身法清净，空明一体，是具备七金刚法自性之身，由地下的地居明妃代表，身（大日如来佛）作为其手势。语喜金刚是佛语的功德在深密修道中所幻化的形象，由于其发出的声音美妙悦耳、赏心可意、悠扬明晰、入耳中听，故名语喜金刚，由居住在天顶的空行母代表，贪（阿弥陀佛）作为其手势。意喜金刚由无我佛母代表，因为心是无我佛母的特质，故居中央。

Sawarui Dakini who holds a monk on her right hand and takes a fan in her left hand. She is in charge of the south-east. She represents the pure and clean water. The fifth one is Bukakasi Dakini. She is blue. She is in charge of the north-east and symbolizes the pure and clean earth. There is a white lion in her right hand and a vajra ax in the left hand. Like Hevajra, every Dakini steps on a person.

Corresponding with the Hevajra Dharma, Hevajra is divided into three kinds: the Body Hevajra, the Language Hevajra and the Mind Hevajra, which masters the underground world, the overground world and the heaven world respectively. The Body Hevajra is the body of illusion and transformation of Hevajra, means all body-dharmas are clean and are the union of light and emptiness. The Dakini living in the underground world acts on behalf of Hevajra. The Language Hevajra was illusorily transformed by Buddha's words when he did yoga. Hevajra gets this name because his sound is deep-lunged and sounds as pleasant as the music. The Dakini living in the heaven is his delegate, and his hand uses greed as his gesture. The Mind Hevajra is represented by the dakini of Vajra-anatman who lives in the middle of the heaven and the underground.

Hevajra Mandala is regarded as a great mandala which is for Hevajra and his followers to get together. Every Dakini has her own position, symbol, color, implements and pedestal. According to *the Collection of Auspicious Hevajra's Dew Spring*, an arched niche for a statue of the Buddha is positioned on each of the two sides of Hevajra on the Mandala. Alongside with him, there are four Dakinis on left and right sides respectively. They are illusorily

喜金刚曼荼罗被视为大曼荼罗，是喜金刚本尊和眷从会合的具体形象的曼荼罗，每一尊天母，各有其所属的方位、蕴义、种字、颜色、持物、台座等。根据《吉祥喜金刚集轮甘露泉》记载，曼荼罗中位于喜金刚本尊两侧方拱形佛龛，左右各有四天母，是吉祥喜金刚足下洁净不染之莲花的八片花瓣所蕴化而生的。每一尊的形象不完全相同，呈现怖畏，象征威镇邪魔，摧碎障蔽；寓意悲智，表示利益众生，证悟大乐。其具体画法，如《喜金刚续第二品》所说：从中央向左右各留半个微度量单位的空间，其间为莲花中心；依次向左右各留五个半微度量单位的空间，其间绘莲花花蕊；依次向左右各留十个微度量单位的空间，其间绘莲花花瓣；最外层左右尚余一个微度量单位的空间，其间绘金刚鬘。

transformed from the eight petals of the clean lotus stepped on by Hevajra. Each of them is different from others, some is fearful to threat demons, some is merciful to help living beings to arrive great joy. The special paint to Hevajra can be seen in *the chapter two of Hevajra Fundamental Tantra*.

五

大威德金刚

Vajrabhairava

大威德金刚
Vajrabhairava

大威德金刚，又译“大威德明王”“怖畏金刚”“牛头明王”，梵文为 Vajrabhairava 或 Yanmantaka，藏文为 RDo-rJe-‘Jigs-Byed，是藏传佛教无上瑜伽部五大本尊之一，因“有伏恶之势，谓之大威；有护善之功，谓之大德”而得名，表现出湿婆神狂暴的一面。佛经说他是文殊菩萨为镇服阎王而化现的忿怒相，此相是事业之本。又说他是西方莲花部无量寿佛的忿怒相。

《时轮根本续》中提到：佛陀在南印度的吉祥聚米塔化现大威德金刚形象和黑阎摩德迦曼荼罗，向金刚手菩萨及无数受用身、化身讲阎摩德迦法。《六面童子续》说：佛调伏忿怒羯摩阎摩德迦、天子、业阎摩、大自在天之后，分别讲《阎摩德迦续》《阎摩德迦黑敌续》《六面童子续》和《九尊大威德续》。《大威德教法源流》说，诛业阎罗王构筑人肉大地、血海、骨山后，损害三界一切有情。这时，色究竟天的诸佛决定从报身寂静妙吉祥（文殊）的心中化现九头三十四臂十六足大威德金刚，来到无色界用身、语、意、事业四种威猛方法调伏无色处四边诸天神，而获遍知位。之后，用同样的方法调伏了色界四种静虑天；在欲界调伏了四天；在三十三天，调伏了居住在须弥山的诸天。

Vajrabhairava or Yamantaka, RDo-rJe-‘Jigs-Byed in Tibetan, is also one of the five great Satyadevatas of Supreme Yoga Tantra in Tibetan Buddhism. Due to Vajrabhairava has the power of subduing demons and protecting good deities, he got his name. Because Vajrabhairava sometimes shows bad temper like Shiva, so Buddhist sutras says that Vajrabhairava is not only illusorily transformed by Manjusri when subduing Yama with the power of wrathful and the basis of enterprise, but also is the wrathful appearance of Amitayus Buddha of the west Padma Family.

In *Kalacakra Fundamental Tantra*, a story describes that Buddha illusorily transformed himself as Vajrabhairava and black Yamantaka Mandala to deliver the Dharma of Yamantaka to Vajrapani and numerous Sambhogakayas and Nirmanakayas. *The Tantra of Six-face Child* tells another story that after subduing angry Karma Yamantaka, devas, Karma Yama and Mahesvara, the Buddha delivered lectures on *the Tantra of Yamantaka, the Tantra of Yamantaka's Black Enermy, the Tantra of Six-face Child* and *The Tantra of Nine Yamantakas*. There is a story in *the Dharma of Yamantaka's Origin and Source* which tells why the Buddha felt that he should subdue these deities. Once there was a horrible time when the Yama made use of people's meat, blood and bones to construct the world, killing living beings. Under this situation, Buddhas living in Akanishtha decided to illusorily transform the three-head, thirty-four-arm and sixteen-feet Yamantaka from the heat of Sambhogakaya of quiet Manjushri. First of all, Yamantaka came to the Arupadhatu to moderate and subdue the deities of Arupadhatu and accomplished the universal knowledge through the four brave and fierce methods, such as the body, the language, the mind and the enterprise. Afterwards, he came to the Rupadhatu to moderate and subdue Four Meditating Deities by the same way. What is

萨迦·三木旦嘉措的《阎摩德迦教法源流》认为：大威德金刚有法身、受用身、化身三种，法身大威德金刚能用无二智慧摧毁一切相状分别；受用身大威德金刚，即寂静文殊像，居住在色究竟天；化身大威德金刚调伏的对象有两部分，一部分是普通的难以调伏的羯磨阎摩，另一部分是忿怒羯磨阎摩，为调伏它们，大威德金刚变化成一头水牛形象，有九头三十四臂十六足，他的每一只手、每一面和每一只眼睛都能调伏包括帝释天、大自在天、遍入天等在内的诸天。

第一世嘉木央协贝多杰的《吉祥大威德金刚教法源流——三界尊胜成就库》认为：一面二臂大威德变化出有十万个头千万只手臂的大威德金刚，獠牙切齿，头发黄竖，犹如太阳火焰，像金刚一样坚不可摧；血盆大口，好像能吞噬三界；眉宇中间的怒纹和双眼，像金刚火一样燃烧，令人目不忍睹；牙齿酷似雪山，獠牙外露，具金刚光。他的特点有：嘱托（禳解病魔）、成就事业、分别调伏、具悲悯心与平等性、为三世诸佛父佛母佛子、使役凶恶者、为大自在天坛城的主尊。也说大威德金刚有十四个特点：一、自生，一面二臂大威德金刚可以根据不同的调伏对象应化相应的形象，以达到调伏的目的；二、顺从安住：被调伏

more, he came to the Kamadhatu to tame four deities. Finally, in the Trayastrimshas, he used the same method to moderate and subdue deities living in Mount Sumeru.

According to *the Origin and Source of Yamantaka Teaching*, Vajrabhairava has three kinds of transformation, namely the Dharmakaya, the Sambhogakaya and the Nirmanakaya. Dharmakaya Vajrabhairava has the power of destroying all appearances and diversities by the fundamental wisdom. Sambhogakaya Vajrabhairava is the quiet Manjushri living in Akanishtha. The demons that the Nirmanakaya of Vajrabhairava subdued can be divided into two types, one being normally hard to be moderated and subdued and the other being Angry Karma Yama. In order to moderate and subdue Angry Karma Yama, Vajrabhairava transform himself as a buffalo with nine heads, thirty-four arms and sixteen feet. Each of his hands, faces and eyes can moderate and subdue deities including Indra, Mahesvara and Vishnu.

In the description of *the Origin and Source of Auspicious Vajrabhairava's Teaching: Successors in Three Worlds*, that Vajrabhairava with ten-thousand heads and ten-thousand arms is transformed from the one-face and two-arms' Vajrabhairava, who is buffalo-like and with long ivory. His erecting yellow hair is just like the flame of sun, which is similar to diamond which cannot be destroyed. He opens his bloody mouth widely, which make people think he can devour all three worlds. No one could bear his eyesight for his eyes burn with angry. His ivory-like teeth are snowy and shining. Some people say that Vajrabhairava specializes in curing illness, enabling success, subduing the heart of distinguishment, representing compassion and equality and

者能遵从调伏者的意愿安顺守己，不再为非作歹，制造障碍，侵袭众生；三、能调伏八大天王到阎罗王之间的所有天魔；四、头发竖起，形象可怖；五、巨型大口，可吞食三界；六、眉间有怒纹，面色发黄似烈火；七、双脚具有威力，可压履世间；八、双手掐期剋印，令世间出世间畏惧而遵从；九、右腿收屈，左腿伸张，能调伏男女八天、男女阎罗（即八男八女阎罗王：黑阎魔、拜雅瓦底、棕密、褐蹄、九股青发、黑白斧、青牛头、褐火曜；信使女、獠牙女、棍杖女、时相女、时绢女、环套女、倒落女、铁钩女）及八种病魔；十、能用遍布天空的八种威猛暴笑降伏梵天等；十一、从本面化现的一切口中能发出"啪""咤"等可怕的诅咒声；十二、以威猛心能做身语二金刚的本性；十三、大威德金刚是变化的形体，大威德是方便，金刚即智慧，空性与大悲无别的菩提心是大威德金刚；十四、在大寒林曼荼罗中，能役使恶魔及阎罗王等，且作为大自在天曼荼罗坛城中的主供本尊，能运用各种神通讲十万经续。

《吉祥大金刚怖畏生起次第安立显耀顶饰》中讲道：大自在天和邬摩天女之子六面童子与阿修罗王楼陀罗在瞻部洲争斗，结果楼陀罗大胜六面童子。这时，大自在天正好住在须弥山阿修罗处，知道自己的儿子战败，于是

doing what Buddhas and their family members want. Some people deem that Vajrabhairava has fifteen features. He (1) is self-born, changes images in accordance with different enemies in order to subdued them, (2) does what he want willingly, stays in obedience and peace, (3) is able to tame every deity and demon, (4) has horrible image with erecting hair style, (5) has huge mouth, as if which can swallow three worlds, and (6)has angry wrinkles between eyes, which is yellow and fire-like, (7)and has powerful feet as if that can cover the world, (8) makes hands in Tarjani gesture for threatening all living beings, (9) stretches his left leg and curving his right leg a little to tame eight kind of male and female deities and eight type of illness, (10) has the power of taming the Mahabrahman by roaring laughters echoing all over the heaven, (11) makes terrible cursing sounds like "bang", "bang", (12) makes brave and fierce heart as the nature of Body Vajrabhirava and Language Vajrabhirava, (13) unifies the wisdom and the method, or shunyata and compassion, and had the ability to achieve great success, and (14) has the power of enslaving demos and Yama in the Great Cemetery Mandala and as the main Satyadevata worshipped in Mahashvara Mandala, delivers thousands of sutras and tantras.

Besides, a war depicted in *the Successive Method of Practicing Auspicious Vajrabhairava* explains the origin of Vajrabhairava. Once upon a time, Six-faces Child, the son of Mahesvara and Deviuma, fought with Rudra, the king of Asura, in Jambudvipa. At last, Rudra won the war. Meanwhile, Mahesvara was visiting Asura in Mount Sumeru and happened to get the news that his son lose the war. He was so angry and immediately headed thirty-three deities and demons from eight sects to beat down Rudra. Rudra had no choice but to escape and seek help from

大威德金刚双身像
The Double-body Statue of Vajrabhairava

率领三十三天的天兵及地上的八部魔军等，打败了阿修罗王楼陀罗。楼陀罗逃到文殊菩萨处求救，文殊菩萨为对治三十三天、地下阿修罗骑众、地上八病八魔和大自在天，分别化现出具有三十四臂、十六足、水牛面和有直立的男根的形象，宣讲金刚怖畏法。这是大威德金刚的来源。

Manjushri. Manjushri illusorily transformed as the thirty-four-arms, sixteen-feet and buffalo-like-face Vajrabhairava to calm down the anger of Mahesvara by telling the Dharma of Vajrabhairava.

Like others, Vajrabhairava also has a single-body and double-body image, which is human's body with buffalo's face. On his head, there is a statue of Manjushri. Figures with two arms, four arms, eighteen arms and thirty-four arms can all be observed

多面多臂大威德金刚

The Vajrabhairava with Many Faces and Many Arms

大威德金刚有单身和双身两种形象，人身牛头（水牛头，类似于古印度教女神朵喀所杀的水牛魔玛喜夏），又有二臂、四臂、十八臂、三十四臂等形象，头顶文殊菩萨像。常见的单身像为三面、六臂、六足，骑乘一头大白水牛。双身像是九头、三十四臂、十六足。九头大威德金刚，代表九种镇压阎魔王的契经，九面代表佛陀的九类教法，正面三个头的中间的头是水牛头，呈蓝黑色，獠牙切齿，三目圆睁，表示无所不见，洞察一切，头上一对锐利的牛角，代表佛教的胜义谛和世俗谛，或幻身与光明，此头象征压服阎王；其上一头为红色，也是獠牙切齿，三目圆睁，鼻孔喘着粗气，十分恐怖，象征食人夜叉；红头顶着黄色的文殊像，头戴宝冠，象征慈善安详。右边三头三面，中间面呈青蓝色，右面呈红色，左面呈黄色，分别表示忿怒、权势和安静。左边三头三面中的中间一面呈白色，右面呈灰色，左面呈黑灰色，分别表示清净、死亡和忿怒。九头中除上头为文殊菩萨像外，其余八头都戴着五骷髅冠，项挂五十颗人头骨串成的项链。经中说大威德金刚身上装饰有人头骨冠、人头项链、人皮裙、人血胭脂，以人血涂眉、骨灰涂身，身呈粉绿色。

大威德金刚的三十四臂，代表菩萨成佛的三十四种

in statues, wall paintings and Tangkas. Normally, his single-body image has three faces, six arms and rides a white buffalo. The double-body image has nine heads, thirty-four arms and sixteen feet. Nine heads mean nine sutras suppressing Yama, nine faces for Buddha's nine kinds of teaching. The right middle face is a buffalo's face, which is in black-blue and has ivory teeth and three eyes opening widely to see and discern everything. The pair of horns on his head symbolizes the ultimate truth and the worldly truth of Buddhism, or the illusory body and light. On the buffalo face, there is a red head also with ivory teeth and three staring eyes, which is extremely horrible and means anthropophagous Demons. Upon the red one is Manjushri, who wears a jewelry crown and looks benevolent and quiet. On the right side, there are three heads, which have a yellow face, a blue face and a red face in the order from the middle to the end and represent anger, power and peace respectively. On the left side, there are also three heads, that is a grey face, a white face and a black face in the same order, which are the symbols of cleanness, death and anger. Apart from the head of Manjushri, other eight heads all wear the five-skull crowns and the necklaces made by fifty beads of human's head. Sutras said that Vajrabhairava normally is ornamented by human-skull crown, human-head necklace, human-skin skirt, human-blood rouge, human-blood mascara, dyed body as pink-green by bone ash.

The thirty-four arms of Vajrabhairava mean the thirty-four ways to be a Buddha. Each of these arms are stretching straightly with a Buddhism instrument held in hand. These instruments are, from the top to the bottom, a knife, a white tank, a vajra, a plastic cutter, a javelin, a crescent ax, a sword, a stick, a bone cane, a dharma wheel, an awl, a dagger and a hand drum and

大威德金刚

Vajrabhairava

单身像（左）
Left:The Single-body Statue

双身像（中）
Middle:The Double-body Statue

双身像（右）
Right:The Double-body Statue

方法。三十四臂向两边伸开，每只手中拿着法器，右边的手自上而下分别持象皮、钺刀、白筒、金刚杵、钩刀、标枪、月斧、剑、箭、法棒、人骨杖、法轮、椎子、匕首、手鼓等，表示向天王、夜叉等挑战。左手自上而下分别持象皮、颅碗、天王头、藤牌、鲜左腿、长绳、弓、人肠、铃、鲜左臂、丧布、三尖矛、炉、颅器、人左臂、军旗、黑布，掌心向上，表示向诸佛菩萨献神饮。大威德金刚怀抱金刚露漩明妃。其十六足压制阎王十六面铁城，象征十六空相。其中右八足弯曲呈弓步，脚踩八天王，象征物为男人、水牛、黄牛、鹿、蛇、狗、绵羊及狐狸，表示八成就。左八足侧伸，脚踩八女明王，象征物为鹫、枭、鸦、鹦鹉、鹰、鸭、公鸡及雁，表示八自在清净。其脚下诸天全是裸体，表示脱离尘垢。

意大利藏学家图齐在西藏阿里的扎布让寺院看到的九面三十四臂十六足大威德金刚像全身为深蓝色，“展左足，屈右足；能吞咽三界；发出‘哈哈’之笑声；卷舌、咬牙、颦眉；眼睛眉毛如劫尽之火；发黄直立；威吓色无色界天众，亦使诸怖畏天众感到怖畏；发出‘啪嗒’之雷音；吞吃人血、肉、髓、脂；头戴五骷髅冠，以十五颗人头鬘为饰；以黑蛇为络腋；耳铛等为人骨所成；大腹、

so on in the seventeen left hands, mean challenging to deities and demons. The seventeen right hands hold an elephant skin, a skull bowl, a head of deva, a shield, a bloody human left leg, a long rope, a bow, a human bowel, a bell, a bloody human left arm, a shroud, a tricuspid spear, a furnace, a skull container, a human left arm, an army flag and a black cloth, mean offering holy beverage to buddhas and bodhisattvas. Vajrabhairava hugs his partner, Dharanibharya Rolangma, with his two main pairs of arms. He makes his eight right legs in the pose of a bow step and steps on a man, a buffalo, a cattle, a dear, a snake, a dog, a sheep and a fox which are the symbols of the eight devas and the eight achievements. He stretches his eight left legs and steps on a vulture, an owlet, a crow, a parrot, an eagle, a duck, a cock and a wild goose which symbolize the eight female fierce guardians of Buddhism and the eight kinds of cleanness.

Tucci, the famous Italian Tibetologist, has seen a black-blue Vajrabhairava which has nine faces, thirty-four arms and sixteen feet in the temple of TSa Pa Rang. He depicted in the vol.3 of *Indo-tibetica* that (this Vajrabhairava) stretched his left feet, curved his right knees, opened his mouth and laughed, erected his yellow hair and threatened all devas in Arupadhatu and made the sound of 'phata', like thunders. He devoured the human meat, marrow and fat, drunk the human blood and wore five-skull crown ornamented with fifteen human heads. He was naked, with a big belly and an erected penis. His eyelash, eyelid, beard and body hair all burned with fire. His main face, with buffalo horns on the head, showed anger, Between the two horns was a yellow face. Sixteen feet symbolized sixteen empties and the red body meant all dharmas have no cause. The erected penis was the symbol of the union of great happiness. Thirty-four arms symbolized the

大威德金刚
Vajrabhairava

大威德金刚

Vajrabhairava

赤体；男根竖立；睫毛、眼皮、胡子、身毛皆如劫尽之火；主面为暴怒、有角之水牛；两角间有一黄面；发髻上竖，表征与五智同体；因驱魔而现怒相；十六足象征十六空；赤红色的身体象征诸法无生；男根竖立象征与大乐同体；三十四臂象征佛教的三十四道品；除灭无明而持刀；因无我见法见而持矛槊；杵象征一心；因灭除罪障而持钺刀；刺棒象征调伏身语；因灭除邪思而持斧；因灭除邪见而持矛；因掌穿妄见而持箭；因牵引而持钩；因灭除业障而持棍；因其自性与菩提心一致而持天杖；因转法轮而持轮；因与第五智一体而持金刚杵；因灭除悭贪而持锤；因能给予宝剑成就等各种成就而持剑；因以大乐表征其劝诫一切如来而持簸鼓；因催请奉行律仪而持盛满鲜血的颅器；以大悲成办众生义利而持梵头；因战胜众魔而持盾；足象征其给予瑜伽士如佛的地位；因绑定般若而持羂索；因胜伏三界而持弓；为了知诸法空性而持肠；铃象征与般若同体；手象征其能成办诸事；尸林碎布象征除灭障碍我们认识诸法无自性的无明暗障；穿于柱上之人象征对诸法无自性想的悟入；（三角形）火灶象征清净光明；鲜人头象征其充满大悲之甘露；以期剋印威吓诸魔；三叉戟象征身、语、意同体；飘动的布片象征诸法如幻；足踏

thirty-four aids to enlightenment. He holds a knife for eliminating foolishness, and holds a spear for the idea of selflessness, holds a pestle symbolizing one pointedness of mind, holds an axe-spears for cleaning away the barriers of sin, holds a stick for taming body and language, holds an axe for eliminating evil thought, holds a spear for removing wrong ideas, holds an arrow for stabbing false ideas, holds a hook for guiding toward, holds a rod for cleaning away the barriers of action, holds a divine stick for his unity heart with self-nature and bodhi heart, holds a wheel for giving sermons, holds a vajra symbolizing the unity of five wisdoms, holds a hammer for eliminating desires ant thirsty, holds a sword for achieve various successes, holds a drum for symbolizing the great happiness and exhorting every buddhas, holds a bloody skull for obeying law and ritual, holds a brahma head for benefiting all living beings, holds a shield for winning all demons, holds a rob for fastening wisdom, holds a bow for taming Three Worlds, holds an intestine for knowing everything will be empty, holds a bell for unifying with wisdom. His hands mean the accomplishment of all enterprises, his feet mean the level of yogis as Buddhas'. The rags in the corpse forest symbolize we realize everything is selfless nature and eliminate the obstacles of foolishness. We understand the dhamma without self-nature through the person who is pierced by a pillar. The triangle stove symbolizes purity and light; the bloody human head symbolizes it full of the sweet dew of great compassion; the gesture tarjani deters all demons; the trident symbolizes the body, the language and the mind become one; the fluttering piece of cloth symbolizes everything is illusion; stepping on a living being means what he gets is the supernatural powers. The Dharanibharya hugged by Vajrabhairava is Vajravetala who is blue and has one face with anger and a pair of arms. She wore

大威德金刚曼荼罗

The Mandala of Vajrabhairava

有情象征由其所得之神通”。（图齐著，魏正中、萨尔吉主编:《梵天佛地》第三卷《西藏西部的寺院及其艺术象征》第二册，上海古籍出版社 2009 年版，第 42~43 页）大威德金刚怀抱着的明妃金刚起尸母全身呈蓝色，一面两臂，呈微怒相，头戴五骷髅冠，项挂十五颗人头骨串成的项链；其右手持钺刀，左手托盛满鲜血的颅器。

清代乾隆时期制作的红铜单尊独雄大威德金刚像的多臂在左右呈扇形展开，右腿屈，左腿伸，整个身体左低右

a five-skull crown and a necklace with fifteen human-head beads. She holds a curved knife in the right hand and a skull container full of blood in the left hand.

The statue of the single-body Vajrabhairava made of copper in Qing Dynasty has all hands stretching out in a fan shape towards the two sides. Its legs are sculpture in a bow pose, with the right leg curving a little and the left stretching straightly. His foot step on eight animals, eight birds, eight male deities and eight female deities. The lotus throne represents the release from samsara, on which there is a sun that means knowing everything. The body is against a backdrop of fire-like sculpture.

大威德金刚曼荼罗
The Mandala of Vajrabhairava

高，足踩八兽、八飞禽、八天三、八女明王。其座下莲花，象征脱离轮回；莲座上有红日，象征如日当空，遍知一切。身后有火焰背光。

另有四面八臂大威德金刚像，上身黄色，下身黑色，项戴人头骷髅链环，腰系虎皮裙。其正面为牛头忿怒相，牙齿外露，舌如闪电，硕大而锐利的牛角显得非常威猛，三只眼圆睁，怒目而视。两边的手持利剑、金刚杵、箭、绳索、弩弓、《般若经》等。

大威德金刚是格鲁派所尊奉的主要本尊，按照他们的说法，十三天曼荼罗中央是主尊大威德金刚，曼荼罗东院

Expect for what is mentioned above, there are also four-face and eight-arm Vajrabhairava which is yellow in the upper part of the body and black in the lower part. He wears a skull-made necklace and a tiger-skin skirt. The middle face is the face of an angry buffalo, which exposes his teeth and thunder-like tongue. The big horns of buffalo are horrible enough to threaten everyone. His third eye is opening widely. He holds swords, vajras, arrows, ropes, crossbows and *the Sutra of Prajna* in his many hands.

Vajrabhairava is the main Satyadevata for the Geluk School to worship. According to the Geluk School, in the Thirteen Deities Mandala, Vajrabhairava is standing at the center. Moha Yamantaka, who is double-body and has three faces and six arms

大威德金刚曼荼罗

The Mandala of Vajrabhairava

是痴阎摩敌。双身三面六臂，身呈白色，三面中主面为白色，左红右蓝；六臂中的左右主臂拥抱明妃，其余左二手分别持珠宝和莲花，右二手持轮与剑。南院为悭阎摩敌，双身三面六臂，身呈黄色，三面中左白右蓝，主面为黄色；左右主臂拥抱明妃，手持钺刀、颅器，其余右二手分别持珠宝、利剑，左二手持法轮、莲花。西院为贪阎摩敌，双身三面六臂，身呈红色，三面之主面为红色，右面蓝左面白；左右主臂拥抱明妃，手持钺刀、颅器，其余四手中的左二手持珠宝、法轮，右二手持莲花、宝剑。北院为妒阎摩敌，双身呈绿色，三面六臂，主面为绿色，其余两面颜色和手持物同贪阎摩敌。东、南、西、北四门分别是锤阎摩敌、

in white skin, manages the eastern yard. The three faces are red, white and blue from the left to the right. He uses the middle pair of his arms to hug his Buddhamatri and the other to hold a jewelry, a sword, a wheel and a lotus respectively The southern yard of the mandala is managed by Matsarya Yamantaka who has yellow body and three faces and six arms, the faces are white, red and blue in the same order as Moha Yamantaka's. His main pair of arms hug his Buddhamatri, which hands hold a knife and a skull container, another two right hands hold a jevelry and a sword, another two left hand hold a wheel and a lotus. The west yard of the mandala is managed by Kama Yamantaka who has double green bodies and three faces, which are in white, green and blue in the same order, and the main pair of arms hug his Buddhamatri, other arms hold with the same instruments as Matsarya Yamantaka in hands. The northern yard of the mandala is Irsya Yamantaka, who is green double-body with three faces, that is blue, green and white, and six

大威德金刚曼荼罗

The Mandala of Vajrabhairava

杖阎摩敌、莲花阎摩敌、剑阎摩敌，都是双身三面六臂。东南、西南、西北、东北四院分别是杂孜噶、亥母、妙音、科日四大天女，身色分别是白、蓝、红、绿，都是三面六臂，手持不同物，各具象征意义。

arms with the instruments in hands. The east, south, west and north gates of the mandala is guarded by Ayoghana Yamantaka, Salaka Yamantaka, Padma Yamantaka and Astra Yamantaka who all have double-body and six arms. White DZa-rTse-Ka Davakanya, blue Pagmo Davakanya, red Sarasvati and green Ke-Ri Davakanya are the protectors of the south-east yard, the south-west yard, the north-west yard and the north-east yard respectively and are all of three faces and six arms with different instruments in hands and has different meaning.

大威德金刚曼荼罗

The Mandala of Vajrabhairava

六

集密金刚

Guhyasamaja

集密金刚
Guhyasamaja

集密金刚，又译“聚密金刚”，梵文为Guhyasamaja，藏文为GSang-Ba‘i-’Dus-Pa，意思是三世诸佛的身、语、意三密无二无别，令聚为集。汉译经典中说他常守候在佛的身边，知道佛的密旨，故名集密金刚。他是藏传佛教无上瑜伽部五大本尊中父续类本尊之一，又是集密教法的名称。其根本经典为《集密根本续》，共十七品。

关于集密法，有许多神奇的传说故事：佛陀在世时，考虑他涅槃以后金刚乘密法如何传承下去，于是每天带领众声闻弟子以法衣作为翅膀，早晨从东方向西方飞，傍晚又从西方飞回东方。有一天，西印度邬仗那国的因陀罗菩提王发现许多酷似黄色的大雁在天空飞行，就问身边的大臣是怎么回事，大臣不知道那是什么，国王又问城中的百姓，才知道是成佛后的净饭王之子和他的声闻弟子在飞行，于是请来佛陀讲解集密法。又说，一次，佛陀与其弟子飞行时被正在宫顶散步的邬仗那自在慧王看见，邬仗那自在慧王问身边的大臣月贤那是什么，月贤回答说可能是大天。自在慧王又问其他侍臣，有人回答说：邬仗那东方有个婆罗奈斯城，净饭王之子悉达多在菩提树下静坐觉悟成佛，佛号“释迦牟尼”，飞行者就是他和他的众弟子。自在慧王十分仰慕，面朝东方不停地祈祷，希望能得到佛陀的加

Guhyasamaja, GSang-Ba‘i-’Dus-Pa in Tibetan, means the union of the body, the language and the mind of three times Buddhas. According to the Chinese Buddhism sutras, Guhyasamaja, who often accompanies Buddha, knows Buddha's secret meaning. Guhyasamaja is one of the five great Satyadevatas of Father Tantra of Supreme Yoga Tantra, and is also the name of the Dharma of Guhayasamaja, of which the basic sutra is *Guhyasamaja Fundamental Tantra*. This sutra has seventeen chapters.

There are many stories about the Dharma of Guhyasamaja. One story says that when Buddha was living in the world, he often thought about how to pass down the Dharma of Guhayasamaja. Finally, he made up his mind. Every day, by transforming their monastic robes to wings, Buddha led his disciples of Sravaka flying from east to west in the morning and from west to east in the evening. One day, Indra Bodhi, the king of the state of Oddiyana in the west of Indian, noticed these flyers. First, the king asked his servants, but he got no answer. Then, he asked his people, they told him that it was Buddha, the son of Shuddhodana, and his followers. Hearing the news, the king invited Buddha to his state to teach the Dharma of Guhayasamaja. Another story has it that, once upon a time, Ishvara Prajna, the king of Oddiyana, was walking on the top of the palace. Suddenly, he found Buddha and his disciples flying over him. He asked the minister beside him and the minister told him that it might be Mahadeva. Then, the king asked his servant, too. The servant answered that in the east of Oddiyana, there was a state named Kapilavastu. Shuddhodana, the king of the state, had a son named Siddhartha who got enlightenment and became Buddha by meditating under a bodhi tree, so he was also called Sakyamuni, meaning the saint of the race of Sakya. Those who were flying in the sky just now were Sakyamuni and his followers. The king of

集密金刚

Guhyasamaja

集密金刚

Guhyasamaja

集密金刚
Guhyasamaja

持。佛陀具有无量神通，得知自在慧王的心愿后，以神变力来到自在慧王的宫殿。国王向佛陀表达了不舍素装，也能成佛的愿望，佛陀满足国王的愿望，设集密曼荼罗，化现金刚持身为其灌顶，讲集密本续法。

集密金刚有寂静和忿怒两种，常见的有彩绘、泥塑和金属铸造的双身像，三头三面六臂。一般主身为深蓝色，代表佛教最高的真理。三头中主头在正中，面呈蓝色，左

Ishvara Prajna admired Sakyamuni so much that he prayed to the east direction continuously for Buddha's aid and support. Buddha immediately knew the king's wishes. He instantly came to the palace of Ishvara Prajna. The king told Sakyamuni his wish to be a Buddha without becoming a monk. Buddha agreed and designated the Mandala of Guhyasamaja to him. When the mandala was finished, Buddha transformed himself as Vajradhara to empower the king, and gave the lecture of tantra of Guhyasamaja.

Guhyasamaja has two kinds of images, the wrathful one and the quiet one. Normally, the many ways of making his image include

集密金刚忿怒相

The Wrathful Appearance of Guhyasamaja

集密金刚
Guhyasamaja

边的面呈红色，右边的面呈白色，每一个头都戴着骷髅冠或五瓣花头冠，顶饰双金刚，象征五方佛或五大菩萨（或五方佛智）。每一面有三只眼，硕大的耳环垂在肩上。六只手臂中，上方两手臂的右手持法轮，左手拿宝珠，分别象征佛法常驻、法轮常转和一切成就。中间两臂（主臂）拥抱明妃金刚佛母，两只手的右手在外，拇指、中指和无名指拿金刚杵，象征方便，其余两指伸直；左手在里，同样用拇指、中指、无名指持金刚铃，象征智慧，金刚杵和金刚铃象征方便智慧双运。下方两手臂的左手持刀，右手拿莲花，分别象征断除一切无明烦恼和智慧清净。双腿跏趺在莲花台上。

集密金刚怀中的金刚佛母三头六臂，全身赤裸，呈浅灰色。其三头仰面，望着本尊，上边两只手臂搂着本尊脖颈；中间二臂上举，拿着法轮；下边二手臂平伸，右手拿着一朵莲花，左手持宝剑；双腿紧勾本尊腰部。佛母和本尊一样，头戴花冠，耳挂大耳环，手腕套着镯子。

由于画派和铸造手法不一样，集密金刚像的风格多种多样，尤其是颜色和背景存在很大差异。清代用青铜铸造的集密金刚像在北京故宫博物院有收藏：金刚跏趺

colored drawings, clay sculptures and metal castings. Guhyasamaja is double-body and has three heads and six arms. The main body is in black blue meaning the highest truth of Buddhism. The three heads are white, blue and red, all wearing a skull crown orfive-pedal flower crown and ornamented by double vajras which symbolize the five great Buddha. Every face has three eyes and huge ears that can touch shoulders. The middle pair of arms hugs Vajra Buddhamatri. The upper right hand holds a vajra, which is the symbol of methods, with the thumb, the middle finger and the ring finger. The upper left hand takes a vajra bell which means wisdom. The vajra and the vajra bell represent the union of method and wisdom. The bottom right hand holds a knife and the left takes a lotus. The knife means cutting all ignorance, while the lotus means clear wisdom. Guhyasamaja sits on the lotus seat in the full-lotus posture.

Vajra Buddhamatri who is hugged by Guhyasamaja also has three heads and six arms. She is grey and naked. Her three heads look up toward Guhyasamaja. The upper two arms embrace his neck, the middle arms holding wheels and the bottom arms taking a lotus and a sword. Her two legs embrace Guhyasamaja's waist tightly. Like Guhyasamaja, Vajra Buddhamatri wears a skull crown, earrings and bracelet.

The different ways of painting and sculpturing make the statue of Guhyasamaja diversified, especially in color and background. In Qing Dynasty, the image of Guhyasamaja was casted by bronze, which is sitting in full-lotus posture on lotus seat, has three angry faces and six arms. Vajrabuddhamatri hugged by him is three faces and six arms, too. Lotus seat is one floor with many floors of lotus pedals. This kind of statue is collected in Beijing Palace Museum.

集密金刚

Guhyasamaja

于莲花座上，三面六臂，呈忿怒相，怀中所抱金刚佛母也是三面六臂；莲座单层，莲瓣多层，瓣尖卷翻。还有缂丝集密金刚像，完全是用经纬丝交织画面，本尊身为蓝黑色，三面六臂，头光呈浅绿色，大红色身光套红黄蓝白四色光环。本尊两侧各有两位大成就者，上方是不动金刚佛。

集密金刚曼荼罗的结构相对比较简单，中央是本尊集密金刚，周围有佛眼菩萨、我母菩萨、白衣母菩萨、救度菩萨等。

There is still a statue of Guhyasamaja made of silk, which uses longitude and latitude thread to paint the Satyadevata who is black-blue with three heads and six arms. The halo around his head is green, the halo around his body is four color circle that are red, yellow, blue and white. There are four Mahasiddhas standing on the Satyadevata's two sides, each sides have two Mahasiddhas. On the top of him is Aksobhyavajra Buddha.

The Mandala of Guhyasamaja is simpler than others, in the center of which is Guhyasamaja with the Buddhalocana Bodhisattva, Mamakibodhisattva, pandaravasini and Tara Bodhisattva around.

集密金刚

Guhyasamaja

集密金刚曼荼罗

The Mandala of Guhyasamaja

集密金刚

Guhyasamaja

七

吉祥天母

Lakshmi

吉祥天母

Lakshmi

吉祥天母，又称“大吉祥天女”“吉祥功德女”“宝藏天女”“威德天女”等，梵文为Lakshmi，藏文为Dpal-lDan-lHa-Mo。吉祥天母俗称“骡子天王”。她是藏传佛教万神殿中居首席的出世间黑色女护法神，也是藏密的护法女神。她源自印度，是佛教和婆罗门教共同的神灵，《大吉祥天女十二契一百八名无垢大乘经》和《佛说大吉祥天女十二名号经》分别提到了其一百零八个和十二个名号。在婆罗门教、印度教中，她是命运、财富、美丽女神，最早见于《吠陀经》之一的《梨俱吠陀——赞颂明论》，到了《阿闼婆吠陀》，她被人格化，有了两种形象，即“吉”与“不吉”，也就是藏传佛教中的寂静和忿怒。在诗史、《往世书》时代，她成为女神，为阳光之神毗湿奴的配偶，成为爱神之母。印度教神话中说她是天神和阿修罗搅乳海时产生的，称“乳海之女”，父亲名为德叉迦，母亲名为鬼子母神。藏文《宝生》一书这样描述：在一个血与脂肪形成的大海中央，吉祥天母从其中的字母bhyo中生出，她骑着白额野马，手持用罗刹头和罗刹皮做装饰的毡带及蛇绳。从她背后的白色bhyo字母中化现喜饶拉姆（智慧女神）女神，全身呈白色，面带微笑，有三只眼，骑在饰有珍贵鞍鞯的白骡子上。从吉祥天母右侧的黄色bhyo字

Lakshmi, DPal-lDan-lHa-Mo in Tibetan, is the chief protector of leaving the world in the Tibetan Buddhism pantheon and also the female protector of the its Tantra. Lakshmi originates from Indian and is worshipped by Buddhists as well as Brahmanists. She has many names, one hundred and eight mentioned in *the Sutra of Great Lakshmi 's One Hundred and Eight Names* and twelve mentioned in *the Sutra of the Great Lakshmi 's Twelve Names*. In Brahmanism and Hinduism, she is the goddess of fates, fortune and beauty. She appeared in the *Rig Veda*, one of the Vedas Sutra, for the first time and was then personalized in *Atharva Veda*. Since then, she has two distinctive images, the auspicious one and the inauspicious one, or the quiet one and the wrathful one in Tibetan Buddhism. In the times of the epic poetry and *Puranas* in Indian history, Lakshmi became a goddess, the wife of Vishnu and the mother of the god of love. The myth of Hinduism says Lakshmi was born during the Churning Milk Ocean event did by devas and Asura. Therefore, she is also called Daughter of the Milk Ocean. Dem-KHra-Ka is her father and 'Dre-Bu-Ma-Mo is her mother. It is described in *Rin-' Byung*, a Tibetan book, that in the center of the ocean of blood and fat, DPal-lDan-lHa-Mo was born in the word of "bhyo". She rode on a wild horse with white forehead, holding a gag rein made by the head and skin of demons. Behind her, Shes-Rab-lHa-Mo appeared from the white word of "bhyo", who was white, smiling and had three eyes, riding on a white mule ornamented by jewelries. From the yellow word of "bhyo" on DPal-lDan-lHa-Mo's left side appeared RGyas-Pa'i-lHa-Mo who had a yellow body giving out yellow light, three eyes and made a full-lotus posture. From the red "bhyo" on DPal-iDan-lHa-Mo's right side appeared DBang-Kyi-lHa-Mo who had an angry face with three eyes, wore red silk dress and shedding red

吉祥天母忿怒相

The Wrathful Appearance of Lakshmi

母中化现杰贝拉姆女神，一身黄色，三只眼，呈盘腿姿势，体内发射出黄光。吉祥天母左侧的红色 bhyo 字母中化现骑着红骡子的旺杰拉姆（自在女神），有三只眼，呈忿怒相，身着红丝衣，体内发出红光。吉祥天母前方深蓝色的 bhyo 字母中化现黑色女神查贝拉姆（忿怒吉祥女神），一面两臂，三只眼怒睁，獠牙切齿，一脸的怒相，毛发如同火焰竖起，她骑在黑色的骡子上，体内发出黑光。吉祥天母的周围还有魔、阎王、罗刹、神、龙、夜叉等，各个手持金刚、战斧、剑刀、矛钩等。印度的一些书中把吉祥天母看成是幸运和财富之神。她就是印度教的最大女神迦梨，具有温柔和可怖的双重属性。

又说吉祥天母出现在创世之时，端坐在一个莲花座上，随水漂流，婀娜多姿，美貌绝伦，使得天神和阿修罗为占有她而发生争执。因为她行为放荡，有上百个情人，父亲非常生气，将她的手脚用铁链锁住关在狗窝里，希望她做个本分的人。母亲疼爱女儿，不愿看着她被铁链锁着，让她悄悄地骑着骡子逃跑。父亲知道后，骑马追赶不及，搭弓射箭，却射中了骡子的屁股。吉祥天母拔下箭，箭孔化成一只眼睛。父亲十分气愤，祈求上苍给女儿最丑

light from her body. Dray-dPal-lHa-Mo made an appearance in front of DPal-lDan-lDa-Mo's black "bhyo". She showed an angry image with three eyes on her face, and her hair was erecting like fire. She rode on a black mule and emitted black light. Around DPal-lDan-lHa-Mo, there were demons, yanas, deities, dragons and yakshas, all of which hold instruments, such as vajras, battle axes, swords or spears etc.Some Indian books regard her as the goddess of luck and wealth. She is the great female goddess Kali with both of the characteristics of gentleness and horribleness.

Another tale depicts that Lakshmi emerged in the time of creation, sitting on a lotus drifting with water. She was so pretty and charming that the devas and Asura were all attracted to her and fought for her. She dated with them all and acted as a dissolute woman. When her father knew her manner, he got so mad as to lock her in a doghouse in order to change her. Lakshmi 's mother can't bear her daughter being tortured and help her escape by riding a mule. After getting the news, the father ran after his daughter by riding a horse. He shot the mule with a bow, and an arrow hit the mule's ass. Lakshmi pulled out the arrow and the hole transformed into eyes. The father was mad as a wet and prayed to the heaven that her daughter shall be given an ugly face. When Lakshmi became ugly, her lover all left her. She had no choice but to wander around. She got acquainted with Raksa and gave birth to two daughters with him. They lived by eating human. When the most infinitely merciful Avalokitesvara knew Lakshmi's story, she warned her to give up harming others and mend her way. Avalokitesvara gave her a sword and ordered her to kill Raksa in one-hundred days. Raksa heard about the order and stayed alert day and night. When sleeping, he always kept an eye open. It was the last day before the

的容貌。吉祥天母变成丑女后，原来的情人纷纷离她而去。因此，她到处流浪，结识了罗刹，两人生下一对女儿，以吃人为生。观世音菩萨得知此事后，警告她不要残害生灵，要改邪归正，并给她一把宝剑，限她百日内杀掉罗刹。魔鬼罗刹知道了此事，昼夜防备，晚上睡觉时总是睁一只眼闭一只眼。就这样，一直到限期的最后一天，吉祥天母摘下天上的月亮吞入肚内，趁黑夜杀死罗刹，在佛的感召下修行成神，下海剿妖。

还说吉祥天母是妙音天女化现的一位忿怒护法女神，被观世音菩萨制服后，列为护法神，作为四大天王毗沙门天的妹妹，因为对众生有大功德，故亦称“功德天”。

苯教文献中提道：吉祥天母是一个专吃人肉、喝人血的空行母，先后上嫁神界，中嫁魔界，下嫁龙界，其右耳朵上挂的狮子耳环和头上的孔雀羽是神界的奖赏，左耳朵挂的蛇是龙界的奖赏。

西藏吉祥天母像出现在吐蕃时期，据载，七世纪时，松赞干布王建成大昭寺后，用自己的鼻血亲自绘制了一幅吉祥天母画，并请她坐镇三楼护法神殿，做大昭寺和拉萨城的保护神。

deadline, Lakshmi picked off the moon, swallowed it and then killed Raksa in darkness. Touched and inspired by the Buddha, Lakshmi became a deity.

Yet another story said that Lakshmi is the wrathful goddess of transformation of Sarasvat. After being tamed by Avalokitesvara, Lakshmi became a deity of protector and the sister of the four great devas. Because of her great contribution to living beings, she was called the Goddess of Fortune.

Based on documents of Bon religion, Lakshmi is a dakini who eats human, married a deity in the heaven, a demon in the devildom and the dragon world one after another. She wears a lion earring on right ear and the feather of a peacock on the head, the prize of the deity world, and a snake earring on left ear which is rewarded by the dragon world.

According to the first record of the appearance of the image of Lakshmi in Tibet, when Srong-bTSan-sGam-Po, the great king, was building the Jokhang Temple, he used his nosebleed to draw a painting of Lakshmi. He put the painting on the third floor of the magnificent building, regarding her as the protector of the temple.

Normally, Lakshmi appears in a single body and has two or four arms. Two-arm Lakshmi stands on a lotus seat and is accompanied by two white elephants, the symbol of auspice. Her one hand takes a lotus and the other is scattering money. She sometimes rides on a garuda bird, sometimes on an owl or a mule. The painting of Lakshmi is one-head with three eyes, orange hair which erects up with crescent ornaments. She wears

常见的吉祥天母像是单身像，有两臂和四臂两种。两臂吉祥天母像，其一手持莲花，一手撒金钱，站在莲花座上，有两只白象伴护，以为吉祥的象征。其坐骑不定，有时是莲花、金翅鸟，有时是猫头鹰、骡子等。一般画像中，吉祥天母为一头三眼，头发橙色，怒而上竖，发饰半月，顶戴五骷髅冠；两手持物，其中右手持金刚棒，左手捧颅碗；脐间有太阳，表示阴性智慧；腰系人皮，上身穿虎皮，表示忿怒；腰间插的三角板专门用来记录人事，凡被记录者剥皮；胯下一头四眼骡子（除了头上有两只眼外，臀部也有两只眼），鞍子用罗刹皮包饰，鞍桥前挂着一口布袋和红白两个骰子，分别用来盛装疾病和主杀赦，鞍桥后有红绿两个线团，触及者即可生病。

由于画派和宗派不同，常见的吉祥天母有寂静相和忿怒相两种。吉祥天母寂静相面色洁白，眉目清秀，双唇微开，双眼有神，闪着和善的目光，额头一眼好像能透视一切；头顶有高耸的发髻和花冠，耳挂大环，左手捧着一只装满珠宝的碗，右手持一支白杆的长羽箭；身披白色大衣，内穿大红袍，脚蹬红靴子，端坐在莲花座上。

吉祥天母忿怒相，面呈蓝黑色，血盆大口，獠牙切齿，

a five-skull crown. She holds a vajra in the right hand and a skull bowl in the left. The sun painted on her navel stands for the female wisdom. She ties a human pelt around her waist and wears a tiger-skin skirt, which shows anger. There is a recorder tied to her waist which is used to make a note of people's actions. Once recorded by her, the person's skin will be peeled off. The mule she rides has four eyes and two of them are on the ass. The saddle is ornamented by the skin of Raksa. There are a bag and two dices hanging on it. The bag is used to pack diseases, while the two dices are red and white, for death and pardon respectively. On the back of the saddle, there are two balls of string, one is red and the other is green. If one touches them, one would catch disease.

Different school of painting draws Lakshmi differently. Generally, there are two kinds of images, one quiet, the other angry. For the quiet one, Lakshmi has delicate complexion with smiling on her face and compassionate flame in her eyes. The third eye on her forehead can discern everything. She wears a flower crown on her bun, and earrings on her ears. There is a bowl full of jewelries in her left hand and an arrow with long bird feather in her right hand. Sitting squarely on a lotus seat, she dresses a red gown and a white overcoat and a pair of red boots.

For the wrathful one, her face is black-blue, her mouth opens widely, her teeth bared, her red nose gasps for breath, her three eyes stare, her eyebrows erect. In a word, this image is horrible enough to scare people away. Erects like a lion, her red hair is ornamented with crescents and the feather of a peacock. She wears a skull crown, a necklace and a pair of earrings. On the left earring, there is a lion which means listening sutras, while on the right earring, there

吉祥天母

Lakshmi

红色鼻孔喘着粗气，三目圆睁，眉毛上竖，令人望而生畏；红色头发竖起，戴着五骷髅冠，火焰形发髻中间有半月和孔雀羽；颈戴多条项链；两耳挂着耳环，右耳环装饰有小狮子，表示听经，左耳环上挂着小蛇，表示忿怒；左手端着盛满鲜血的颅器，表示幸福快乐，右手持骷髅棒，用来对付阿修罗。传说她身上披着她儿子的皮，表示大义灭亲。她骑着黄色骡子，表示她可以在天上、地上、地下三界行走自如。

清代吉祥天母画像，相貌丑陋，狰狞可怖，右手高举红色金刚头杖，左手拿着盛满鲜血的颅器，斜跨在黄色骡子上，在血海中奔走。其背景是集密金刚、大威德金刚和胜乐金刚像。藏文文献记载，吉祥天母的装束有八种：鳄鱼威武装束，神采奕奕；日月双轮装束，表示方便智慧合一；智慧火装束，表示烧毁一切烦恼毒害；新月獠牙装束，表示根除生死源头；金刚翅装束，表示实现一切愿望；金刚装束，表示具备权威；红铜甲装束，表示是入解脱处之王；黑乌铁甲装束，表示禳灾除邪。因此，她被奉为众神之首、众佛之母，既是藏传密法的保护神，也是拉萨地区的保护神。她有上百个化身，形

is a snake which means anger. The vajra held by left hand is for fighting Asura, while the skull container took by right hand is the symbol of happiness. It is said that the cover she wears is the skin of her son, which means placing righteousness above family loyalty. The yellow mule, the ride of the angry Lakshmi, means she can travel freely in the three worlds, the heaven, the underground and the man's world.

In the painting of Lakshmi of the Qing Dynasty, she is extremely ugly and horrible. Riding on a yellow mule traversing in the blood ocean, she lifts a red vajra cane in right hand and holds a skull bowl full of blood in left hand, with Guhyasamaja, Vajrabhairava, Cakrasamvara around. According to the documents of Tibet, Lakshmi has eight kinds of suits, including the crocodile suit in fine fettle, the suit of the double wheel of sun and moon symbolizing the union of method and wisdom, the suit of the fire of wisdom symbolizing burning down all annoyances, the crescent-tusk suit symbolizing eliminating the root of birth and death, the vajra-wind suit symbolizing the realization of all wishes, the vajra suit symbolizing the power, the suit of red bronze armor symbolizing the king of release and the suit of black iron armor symbolizing the remove of disasters and evils. Because of her possession of these merits and virtues, she is not only regarded as the chief of all deities and the mother of all Buddhas, but also the protector deity of Tibetan Buddhism and the area of Lhasa. Lakshmi has hundreds of different transformations. LHa-Mo-Lags Lake, in Jiacha County of Shannan Prefecture, is seen as Lakshmi's spirit lake and the place for finding the reincarnated soul boy of the living Buddha. It is said in legends that the lake

象各不一样。山南加查县内的拉姆拉措湖被看成是她的魂湖，是寻找活佛转世灵童时必去的地方之一——传说湖水可以显现出灵童出生的方位和周围的环境，久而久之，人们便形成了选灵童观湖的习惯。

西藏勉唐画派所画的吉祥天母像，其身体是用焚烧尸体的灰烬涂裹而成的，她肌肉隆起的四肢表达着她的愤怒与力量，面部表情奇特而夸张，三只怒目暴睁，竖立的眉毛像燃着的红色烈火，大张的血口龇出凶狠的白牙，口中咬着一横卧的人，鼻孔扁平，涂红色。女神手指、脚趾都长着尖尖的爪钩，其右手挥舞着一根巨大的饰有金刚杵的檀木杖，象征她摧破魔障的法力，左手在胸前托捧着一盛满血浆的头骨碗，藏语称嘎巴拉，据说那头骨碗中装的是从乱伦所生的孩子身上取出的童血，这一法器更代表了女神空行怒尊的大功力。女神身穿丝质飞动般的黑色衣裙帛带，头戴五骷髅骨制成的头饰，颈挂用十五个鲜人头颅串成的大花环，腰系长蛇缠绕的腰带，一缕一缕的长发在她头顶直立飞冲，上承一孔雀羽毛扎成的宝冠，像华盖一样示以威严。女神耳配大耳环，左耳挂青蛇，寓意忿怒，右耳挂一白狮子，表示她听闻佛道。

could show the place and the environment of reincarnated soul boy, so watching the lake is becoming a custom for the selection of the reincarnated soul boy.

In the Lakshmi painting drawn by the Miantang Painting school, her body is made of the ash of burnt corpse; her flexed muscles on the arms and legs shows the power of angry; her countenance is strange and exaggerated. She opens three glaring eyes widely, erects her eyebrows like the red fire, opens her mouth in which one can see a human held in it and has a flat red nostril. Lakshmi's hands have long nails, her right hand is holding a big vajra wood cane which is the symbol of the magic power of destroying evil, while her left hand is taking a skull bowl full of blood which is said to come from a incest baby. The skull bowl means the power of her angry. She wears a black silk dress, a five-skull crown, a fifteen fresh-head necklace, a pair of earrings made of a big black-snake and a white lion head, a snake belt and bracelets, anklets and bangles. The black snake earring means the anger while the white lion head means the dharma of Buddha. Her belly button is ornamented by sun which is the symbol of wisdom. All those ornaments emphasize her noble identity. The typical instrument of Lakshmi is an account book hanging on her waist for recording the bad persons and the evils they did. Besides the book, there are a bag and two dices. The bag is packed with diseases, while the two dices are red and black which are used to judge people's life and death. The yellow mule that she is riding has three eyes, the third of which is on its ass. The human skin on her shoulder makes the painting seems extremely horrible. It is said that the skin is that of her son, meaning placing righteousness

吉祥天母寂静相

The Quiet Appearance of Lakshmi

其肚脐上饰有红色太阳，喻其智慧。其手镯、脚镯、臂钏、璎珞等庄严一应俱全，强化了女神的尊严和神格的高贵。她典型的法器是腰间挂着的一账簿，以记录恶人恶事，别有一拘魔牌和装有病瘟的口袋及判别生杀的骰子，这些均是女神法力的象征物。她的坐骑即是那匹臀部有一只眼睛的黄色骡子。她肩披倒挂的人皮，让画面更恐怖，然而那又是一种寓意——据说那是她亲生儿子的人皮，表示她为护法可大义灭亲。黄色骡子的双耳直立，双目炯炯，以绿色毒蛇为缰绳和鞧绳，昂首踏行在充满油脂、骨骸的血海中，以此象征吉祥天母具有使修持者免除厄运与悲苦之力。熊熊燃烧的烈火、风烟，随主尊头发、衣带的飘动，营造出一派鏖战激行的气势。骡前骡后，即本尊画像右左各有一侍从引护：右为蓝色空行母，赤裸身体，佩戴璎珞，面如海龙形，手牵蛇缰作引领状；左为深红色空行母，赤身，面如狮形，右手举钺刀，左手托脑骨碗作紧随状。前者象征大海、河流中的一切生物，后者象征陆地、高山，这一切都在她们的掌控之下，表示出女神吉祥天母掌管天上、地上、地下三界的巨大威力，因此她又被称为“三

above family loyalty. The yellow mule with erecting ears, bright eyes and a green snake rein, raises its head and walks in bloody ocean which is full of bones and fat. This scene indicates that Lakshmi protects the yogis from the harm of misfortunes and sufferings. On the back of the powerful deity, the burning fire and smoke are flying with Lakshmi's hair and clothes, as if one could hear the sound of "zi", "zi"... creating the atmosphere of a battle. There are two servants standing on the two sides of mule. The right one is a blue dakini with a naked body and a sea dragon face. The left one is a deep red dakini which is also naked and has a lion face with a battle-knife in right hand and a skull bowl in left hand. The former is the symbol of all sea creatures, while the latter is the symbol of land and mountains. Above all, all these symbols put together signifies the power of Lakshmi to manage all the three

界总主”。在本尊的正下方，一尊头有高发髻、佩戴花冠、面相善慈、目光和悦，身着右衽交领大袍，静坐在水莲之上，右手持长杆羽箭，左手端捧一盛满珠宝的大碗，这个是吉祥天母的寂静相，称为“白拉姆”。在本尊的头上、下方及两侧绘有二十一尊骑乘不一的女神像，其线条轻淡细微、隐约而细密，似在云水中行走、飞行。

大昭寺三楼东侧有吉祥天母护法殿，内有其忿怒相；台阶拐弯处放着传说是她两个女儿的白拉白东玛像和白拉姆像。白拉白东玛是吉祥天母的大女儿，长相丑陋，却很多情，曾和随文成公主护送释迦牟尼十二岁等身像来吐蕃的战神赤宗赞相恋，吉祥天母知道后坚决反对，一气之下把赤宗赞赶到拉萨河南岸，不让两人见面。小女儿白拉姆的画像肤色呈白色，头上有高耸的发髻和花冠，耳朵上坠着大环，三只细长的眼睛流露出和善的目光，嘴微微张开，左右手分别拿着盛满珠宝的碗和白杆长羽箭。传说她好吃懒做，被母亲赶到八廓街接受人们的施舍。也有说二女儿即东赞杰姆（八廓街东南隅的石头画像），在八廓街靠人们的供养为生。实际上，这两位女儿是吉祥天母的两种代表，白拉姆是吉祥天母的寂静相，白拉白东玛是其忿怒相。

worlds, so she is called the head master of the three worlds. Under the angry Lakshmi, there is a quiet image of her. She is elegant and benevolent and wears a traditional Han-style robe. Sitting on the lotus seat peacefully, she holds a long arrow in the right hand and a bowl full of jewelries in the left hand. Because of her quiet image, she is also called white Lha-mo. Except as mentioned above, there still are twenty-one female deities around the main deity, some of them flying and some walking on the water.

Lakshmi Hall was built in the third floor of Jokhang Temple. The sculpture of Lakshmi is the wrathfu one. In the turning of steps, there are the statues of DPal-lHa-dPal-gDong-Ma and DPal-lHa-Mo. Tibetan story says that DPal-lHa-dPal- gDong-Ma and DPal-lHa-Mo were Lakshmi's daughters. DPal-lHa-dPal- gDong-Ma was the eldest daughter who was ugly but full of affection. She fell in love with Grib-rDZong-bTSan, a man good at battles and was following Wen Cheng princess to Tibet. Lakshmi was very much against the love. She expelled Grib-rDZong-bTSan to the south bank of Lhasa River and ordered them to never see each other again. DPal-lHa-Mo was her youngest daughter who was so lazy that her mother expelled her to the east Barkhor Street to live on begging. In fact, the two daughter was no one other but Lakshmi herself. They are the two images of her, the quiet one and the wrathful one.

In the area of Lhasa, the first day of the first month in the Tibetan calendar is regarded as Lakshmi's remember day, on which it is said that she is riding the sunlight to travel around the world. October 15, according to the Tibetan calendar, is the day

吉祥天母

Lakshmi

在拉萨地区，藏历每年的正月初一为吉祥天母的祭日，这天是她骑乘阳光周游世界之日。另外，藏历十月十五日是她与丈夫见面的日子，因此形成了白拉日卓节。按照传统做法，十四日晚，木鲁寺僧人来到大昭寺护法殿迎请吉祥天母像至释迦牟尼佛殿，放在释迦牟尼佛对面。十五日清晨，日出东方时，僧众抬着吉祥天母像，随着长号声绕八角街一圈，行至南大街拐角处时停留片刻，让女神和拉萨河对岸的情人赤宗赞隔河相望。待全部仪式结束后，再将女神像抬回大昭寺供放在原来的宝座上。

she dates with her husband, so the day is called the DPal-lHa-Ri-Grol holiday. Traditionally, at night on Oct 14, monks who come from Me-Ru-dGon-Pa Monastery go to Jokhang Temple's Dharmapala Hall to invite the statue of Lakshmi to Sakyamuni Hall and put her in a position facing Sakyamuni. In the morning of Oct. 15, when the sun arises from the east, monks lift the statue of Lakshmi and walk along the Barkhor Street in a full round in the sound of trombone. When the team arrives at the south corner of the street, they will stop for a while to let the deity and her lover, Grib-rDZong-bTSan see each other. When the ceremony is finished, the statue of Lakshmi is brought to her own seat in Jokhang Temple.

八

大黑天

Mahakala

大黑天
Mahakala

大黑天，又称为“大黑”“大时”“大黑神”等，梵文为 Mahakala，藏文为 Nag-Po-GHen-Po，“Nag-Po”意为“黑”“GHen-Po”意为“大”，“Nag-Po-GHen-Po”意为“大黑”。据说，公元十一世纪，古格王朝时期的著名学者仁钦桑布（宝贤）第一次将大黑天信仰带到西藏，大黑天逐渐成为藏传佛教的重要护法神，位居大护法神之首，同时也是修炼密法所依止的本尊。传说，大黑天是古印度教湿婆神的化身。湿婆神有多种不同的形象，作为破坏神时“面目狰狞，性格狂暴，颈挂骷髅，经常住在墓地，游荡于鬼灵之间，管理死者的时限”。当他毁灭世界时，显现十分可怖的黑色面相。所以，藏密把他看成是大自在天的化身，也是观世音菩萨化现的大护法神。

噶举派著名学者乌坚林巴说：大黑天原是普贤佛教化后期生活在吉域的人，由于受密法感化，出家受戒，法号塔巴那波（黑解脱）。但他骄傲自满，耽于虚妄，经常做杀生、偷盗、邪淫、妄语、两舌、恶口、绮语、贪欲、嗔恚、邪见十恶之事，不断轮回于旁牲道，直至燃灯佛之末期才转世为人，生于罗刹国，三头六臂四足，每个头上有三只眼，身上还长有两只翅膀。当地人把他和他的母亲逐至荒林，他靠吸食自己母亲的血肉存活。长大后，他的三个头的颜

Mahakala, Nag-Po-CHen-Po in Tibetan, means the great black savior. Nag-Po means black, GHen-Po means great. It is said that Mahakala was first introduced to Tibet in the 11th century by Rin-CHen-bZang-Po, the famous scholar of Gurge Kingdom. Since then, Mahakala gradually became the most important and chief protector deity of Tibetan Buddhism and the Satyadevata of Tibetan Tantra. A legend about Mahakala says that Mahakala is transformed by Shiva, one of the three most important deities of Hinduism. Shiva has various appearances. As the Destroyer, Shiva has a horrible face and a rageful and furious personality. He wears a skull necklace, lives in the cemetery, wanders amongst ghosts and spirits and manages the deadline of the living being's life. When Shiva decides to destroy the world, he will show a terrific black appearance. So, Tibetan Tantra sees him as the transformation of Mahashvara and the great protecting deity of the transformation of Avalokiteshvara.

Ao-rGyan-gLiang-Pa, a famous scholar of Kagyu school, believes Mahakala who was a person lived in the Indian area in the end of the time of Samantabhadra Buddha's teaching adopted a monastic life, received ordination and got the dharma name, THa-Ba-Nag-Po, due to the influence of the tanra. However, Mahakala was so conceited and self-satisfied, engaging in ten bad behaviors, that is killing, stealing, adultery, lying, double-tongue, filthy language, improper remarks, greed, anger and holding wrong views. That he was reincarnated again and again as animals. It was not until the end of the time of Dipamkara Buddha that he reincarnated as a person and lived in the state of Raksa. Due to his strange appearance, that he had three heads, each with three eyes, and had six arms, two wings and four feet, he and his mother were expelled to a barren forest by local people. He survived by eating her mother.

色不一样，右面白色，左面红色，中间面蓝色，颈挂骷髅项链，在罗刹国作恶多端，人称玛占嘎如。战胜刹土空行和须弥山的白幢后，他改名叫茹扎，本性不改，继续作乱，佛陀令观世音菩萨和度母分别化成马头金刚和金刚亥母去收服他，让他做佛教的护法神，密号摩诃迦罗。东密认为大黑天是大日如来佛降魔时所化现的忿怒相。他有四大功德，一是他有无数鬼神眷属，个个能飞行隐身，在战争中能保护众生，故名“战神”；二是他能保证众生食物丰足，故名“厨房神”；三是他与眷属七母女天，赐福于贫穷者，故名“福德神”；四是他能经常保护亡人之墓，故名“冥府神”。《佛说摩诃迦罗大黑天神大福德自在圆满菩萨陀罗尼经》说：“尔时，如来告大众言：‘今此大会中，有大菩萨，名曰大福德自在圆满菩萨，此菩萨往昔成等正觉，号大摩尼珠王如来，今以自在业力故，来娑婆世界，显大黑天神。’是大菩萨，大会中，即起座合掌，白佛言：‘我于一切贫穷、无福众生，为与大福德，今现优婆塞形，眷属七母女天，三界游现，欲与众生福德。”

大黑天的身形比较多，常见的有单身二臂、四臂、六臂等，几乎没有双身像。二臂大黑天被看成是普贤佛所化现的智慧护法，能帮助修行者入证空性，其形象为全身黑

As he grew up, his three heads turned into different colors, the right side being white, the left side red, and the middle one blue. He did a lot of bad things and got the nickname of Ma-Bran-Ka-Ru. After Mahakala beat down a dakini of Kshetra and White Pennant of Mount. Sumeru, Ma-Bran-Ka-Ru was renamed as Ru-Dra. A leopard cannot change its spots. Mahakala continued to harm others. Buddha ordered Avalokiteshvara and Tara to transform themselves as Hayagriva and Vajravarahi to subdue Mahakala. Finally, Mahakala became a dharma protector of Buddhism, named Mahakala. In the eastern esoteric sect, Mahakala is seen as the angry appearance of Vairocana Buddha and has four great contributions. Firstly, he has countless ghosts and deities following him, they all can fly and hide themselves. Because he and his followers can protect living beings from harms in wars, so he gets the name of Mars. Secondly, he can bless all living beings with abundant food, so he is called the Deity of Kitchen. Thirdly, he and his family members, the devakanies of seven wives and seven daughters, can help the poor, so he gets the title of the Deity of Good Fortune. Fourthly, he can protect tombs, so has the reputation of the Deity of Hell. In *the Tantra of Buddha said Mahakala's Great Merit and Perfect Bodhisattva* shows that, in that time, Buddha told his follows that there was a Bodhisattva in here today, his name is the Great Merit and Perfect Bodhisattva. He had become a Buddha in the past time and be called the Tathagata of Great Moni King. Now he came to the Soha World, appeared as Mahakala. At that time, the Bodhisattva stood out with holding hands, and said to Buddha that I appeared as normal man for giving the poor people and unluck people blesses. My seven wives and daughters with me traveled around three worlds for bringing blesses and merits to all living beings.

The image about Mahakala is various. Normally, there are

大黑天

Mahakala

大黑天

Mahakala

色，矮小健壮，勇猛力大；四臂大黑天是胜乐金刚的护法；六臂大黑天是千手千眼观世音菩萨和十一面观世音菩萨的化身，能降伏末法时期恶化的众生，帮助众生实现愿望。

从材质上看，大黑天像有布画像、壁画像、泥塑像、金铜质像和铁质像等。一头二臂大黑天，身呈深蓝色或青黑色，三目圆睁，怒目而视，獠牙切齿，两个虎牙外露，呈忿怒相，象征无畏无惧，降伏心魔。他棕色的毛发竖起，头戴五骷髅冠，顶有一尊佛；两臂在胸前，左手托着一只骷髅碗，碗内是翻腾的血水，右手持一把钺刀，做出在碗里搅动状，两臂上横置一根木梃杖；腰系虎皮裙；两腿粗短，做出蹲踞姿势，脚踩一仰卧男人，象征拔除死亡的一切业障；全身挂满瓔珞珠饰，缠着翻动的飘带；画像背光是喷射的火焰，周围有其他佛、空行、护法等，代表大黑天神的眷属。

萨迦派的大黑天造像体形矮小肥大；两肘上横置的杖刀中藏有无数神兵；身披用六种骨珠、瓔珞、蛇、珠宝装饰的衣服；其上方为大鹏，右侧为黑色鸟，左侧为青色铁狼，前方为黑人，后方为黑犬。每一个表情、动作、法器、服饰都有其象征意义。

一头四臂大黑天，全身黑色，黄红色的头发竖起，头戴五骷髅冠，三目圆睁，眉毛上翘，龇牙咧嘴，怒目俯视，

images of one head with two arms, four arms or six arms, but the double-body image is rare. Two-arm Mahakala, which is black, short and powerful, is regarded as the wisdom dharma protector transformed by Samantabhadra Buddha. He can help yogis to prove and enter sunyata. Four-arm Mahakala is the dharma protector of Cakrasamvara. Six-arm Mahakala is the transformation of thousands-hand, thousand-eye and eleven-face Avalokitesvara. He can subdue living beings in the final stage of the spreading of Buddhism and can help their wishes coming true.

The materials for creating the statue of mahakala are many. There are fabric statues, wall paintings, clay statues, gold statues and iron statues. The one-face and two-arm statue of Mahakala is in black-blue color, with three big glowering eyes, exposing teeth and an angry face, symbolizing fearlessness and the subduing of demons in one's own heart. His hair is brown and erecting on his head on top which there is a five-skull crown and a Buddha's statue. His left hand

大黑天

Mahakala

四臂大黑天
Four-arm Mahakala

呈恐怖之相。他项挂人头骨串成的念珠；腰系虎皮裙；四只手中的前两手置胸前，一手持骷髅碗，一手持钺刀，后两手分别置于身体两侧，一手持三股叉，一手持宝剑；两腿向内弯曲，做出游戏状，脚踏两个异教徒。画中大黑天护法神上下各有六尊像，左右两侧也各有三尊，共十八尊，都是他的化身。

holds a skull bowl full of blood, while the right hand takes a knife which seems to be stirring the blood in left hand. His legs are short and make a squat pose, one foot stepping on the body of a man which means the elimination of all elements of death. He wears a tiger-skin skirt and is ornamented by jewelries. The background is burning fire. He is always surrounded by other Buddhas, dakinis and protectors.

The Sakya sect creates their Mahakala as a fat and short statue, which wears six kinds of bone-bead clothes. The cane held

一头六臂大黑天

One-head and Six-arm Mahakala

一头六臂大黑天身呈青黑色，和二臂、四臂一样，三目圆睁，咧嘴露齿，面部表情凶残且呈强笑状，眉毛和头发都是黄褐色；左右各有三只手臂，右边上手高举砍刀，中间手持如意宝珠，置于胸前，下边手紧握人头鼓，左边上手托着盛满甘露并有珍珠的颅器，中间一手挥舞三叉戟，下方的手持绳索；身着杂色丝衣，挂满骷髅、璎珞，腰系虎皮裙，背有象皮护甲，为大日如来佛的忿怒相。

藏传佛教每一个宗派都尊崇大黑天神，并且其本身化现的就多达七十五种身形，因此造像也不尽相同。就六臂大黑天说，除上述形象外，还有一种“身披着一张白象皮，象头朝下，四腿搭在两肩和双腿后。最上右手向上抓着象脚，左手拿三叉戟，中间两只手之右手拿骷髅鼓，左手拿索子，主臂两手仍拿骷髅碗和钺刀。……脖子上还有青蛇、项链，脚脖和手腕上环缠着白蛇，象征着把龙王和药叉都降伏，腰间仍围着虎皮裙，环绕着颗颗人头”。（金申著：《喇嘛庙——佛的世界》，四川民族出版社 1992 年版，第 93 页）

《西藏的神灵和鬼怪》中说：六臂大黑天身呈蓝黑色或黑色，一面三眼六手；面呈暴怒相，张着大嘴，獠牙

by him horizontally between his elbows hides numerous divine armies. Above him, there is a garuda bird. On his left side, there is a black bird, while on his right side, there is a blue iron wolf. Each of these expressions, actions, instruments and dresses have its symbolic meaning.

One-head and four-arm Mahakala also has black body but erecting red-yellow hair. He wears a five-skull crown, a human-skull necklace and a tiger-skin skirt. He opens three eyes widely with a fierce look. Two of the four arms are in front of the chest, one hand holds a skull bowl and the other holds a knife. The other two arms are on his two sides, one hand takes a three-tined fork, the other hand takes a sword. His feet step on two heretics. In the painting of Mahakala, there are eighteen Satyadevatas, which are all the transformations of Mahakala.

Single-body and six-arm Mahakala has the same expression as two-arm or four-arm Mahakala, although the six-arm one is in cyan color. His six arms all hold dharma instruments which are a chopper, a piece of felicitous and precious jewelry, a human-head drum, a skull container, a trident and a rope. He wears silk clothes ornamented by skulls, a tiger-skin skirt and an elephant-leather armor. His face makes a wrathful appearance of Vairocana.

Although Tibetan Buddhism has different schools, all of them make worship to Mahakala. Besides, Mahakala has seventy-five kinds of transformations, so different schools have different statues of Mahakala. There is also another statue which wears a white elephant skin. The head of elephant is toward to ground, the four legs of it put on Mahakala's two shoulders and two legs. His right

外露，舌头向后卷起；头发上缠绕一条蓝色小蛇；右边三手中的上面的手持镶嵌金刚杵的大刀，中间的手持颅骨念珠，同时还抓着身后的象皮，最下面的手挥舞人头骨，左边主臂置胸前，手持装满鲜血的人头骨碗，中间的手持三叉戟，同时抓着另一块象皮，下面的手挥舞两端缠有金刚杵的绳套；脚踏白色的象头神或被击败的生障魔；用绿丝

hand holds the elephant's one foot, left hand holds three-tined fork, the middle two hands hold skeleton drum and rope respectively, the two main hands hold skull bowl and moon knife. A blue snake and a neckless are around his neck, white snakes around his legs and arms, which symbolizes the taming of Dragon King and Yaksa. He wears a tiger-skin skirt and use people heads around his waist. He stretches his left leg and bends his right leg a little.

Deities, Ghosts and Monsters in Tibet says that six-arm Mahakala is

带系着虎皮做围裙；身上缀满各种饰物，手上脚上戴有手镯和脚镯串铃，颈部和头戴绿色项链、红色耳环、人骨饰物、五骷髅头冠和新近剥下的五十颗人头缀成的花冠。

还有一种大黑天叫主寿大黑天，是双身像，一面六臂，身为靛蓝色，须眉犹如燃烧的火焰，竖起的头发呈棕黄色，头戴五骷髅冠，耳挂大耳环。其面部左边白色，右边红色，代表善恶报应。主寿大黑天的两只主臂拥抱灰蓝色明妃（传说那是吉祥天母），手拿铃杵，其余四手各持器物。除这种大黑天像外，其他地方还有少见的八臂、十二臂、十六臂像等。大黑天传入西藏的时间比较早，藏传佛教形成后，大黑天受到宁玛派、噶举派、萨迦派、觉囊派和格鲁派的尊崇，其中萨迦派尊奉一面二臂大黑天，噶举派和格鲁派分别尊奉四臂和六臂大黑天。尽管各派所供奉的大黑天的基本形象没有多大变化，但在形态上有细微差别，而他最大的特点是斜颈、突腹、大头、短腿。

black or blue-black body, has one face, three eyes and six hands. His face expresses very angry, opens his mouth largely, exposes his teeth, and his tongue rolls back. A blue snake is around on his hair. The right three hands hold a broadsword with diamonds, a skull rosary and his robe made by elephant skin, and human skull respectively. The left three hands hold a human skull fulling of blood, a trident and his robe, a robe with diamonds on it. He steps on the deity's head, which is elephant head, or steps on the monster who prevent birth. He uses a green silk ribbon to tie a tiger-skin skirt aground his waist. His body decorate with lots of ornaments, he wears bracelets on arms and legs, and a green necklace around his neck, red big earrings, five-skull crown, and fifty human heads made garland.

Except for what are mentioned above, there is a double-body statue of Longevity Mahakala which has one face and six arms and is in indigo color. His beard and eyebrows are red which seem like flaming fire. He wears a five-skull crown and big earrings, one of earrings being white on the left and red on the right, which means rewards and retributions. The main pair of arms hugs blue dakini, somebody thinks who is Lakshmi. Longevity Mahakala holds vajra and bell. The rest four hands hold different instruments. There are eight-arm, twelve-arm and sixteen-arm statue in some places in Tibet, but they are very rare. Because Mahakala worship spreading to Tibet very early, when Tibetan Buddhism formed, Mahakala is worshipped by a lots of Tibetan Buddhist school, such as Nyingma School, Sakya School, Jonang School, Kagyu School and Gelug School. In them, Sakya School worships one-face and two-arm Mahakala, Kagyu School worships four-arm Mahakala, Gelug School worships six-arm Mahakala. Though, the Mahakala is almost the same appearance for worshipping by these different schools, there still has differences.

六臂大黑天

Six-arm Mahakala

宁玛派四臂大黑天双身像

Double-body Mahakala of Four Arms Worshiped by Nyingma School

六臂大黑天

Six-arm Mahakala

四臂大黑天

Four-arm Mahakala

噶举派大黑天像

Mahakala Worshiped by Kagyu School

新门塘派的大黑天寂静相

The Quiet Appearance of Mahakala Created by Mentang School

大黑天寂静相

The Quiet Appearance of Mahakala

九

金刚亥母

Vajravarahi

金刚亥母
Vajravarahi

金刚亥母，藏传佛教的重要护法神之一，胜乐金刚的明妃，被噶举派奉为本尊，梵文为 Vajravarahi，藏文为 RDo-rJe-Pag-Mo，意译为“金刚母猪”。传说她是古印度教三大主神之一的毗湿奴的化身。毗湿奴（又作“毗瑟怒”“韦纽”，意为“遍入天”）与梵天、湿婆并称为婆罗门教和印度教三大神，最早见于《吠陀经》之一的《梨俱吠陀》——说其三步能跨越地、空、天三界。到了《梵书》和《摩奴法典》中，其特征有所发展，逐渐成为地位仅次于梵天的第二大神。毗湿奴皮肤呈深蓝色，四只手分别拿着法螺、轮宝、仙杖和莲花，象征着虚空的声音、无限时间、摧毁一切仇敌的力量和清净等。她躺在巨蛇身上，漂浮在海上，肚脐上长有一朵莲花，上面坐着梵天。她平时温和，发怒时非常可怖，坐骑是金翅鸟。

毗湿奴的化身除了金刚亥母外，据《薄伽梵往世书》记载，她有鱼、龟、野猪、人狮侏儒、持斧罗摩、罗摩、黑天、佛陀、白马九个重要的化身。《薄伽梵往世书》中说，恶魔毗罗尼亚戈娑把大地沉入大海，眼看着世界将要消亡，毗湿奴化现为一头野猪，潜入海中杀死恶魔，把大地拉了上来。也说毗湿奴的明妃跋罗西以野猪的扮相出现，被佛教吸收后成为护法神，属于出世间空行母。从法理上说，

金刚亥母单身像

The Single-body Statue of Vajravarahi

金刚亥母
Vajravarahi

Vajravarahi, RDo-rJe-Pag-Mo in Tibetan, is one of the important dharma protectors in Tibetan Buddhism, and the Dharanibharya of Cakrasamvara, worshipped as a Satyadevata by Kagyu school. It is said that Vajravarahi is transformed by Vishnu. Vishnu, Brahmadeva and Shiva are the three main deities of Hinduism. Vishnu made its first appearance in *Rig Veda*, which is one of the *Veda Sutra*. According to *Rig Veda*, Vishnu can cross the three worlds of the earth, the empty and the heaven in three steps. In *Brahmana* and *Manu Smriti*, Vishnu gradually developed as the second main deity in Hinduism, only ranked behind Brahmadeva. He is in deep blue color and holds, in the four hands, a conch of dharma, a Chakravartiraja's wheel, a divine cane and a lotus which are the symbols of the empty sound, the limitless time, the strength to destroy everything and the cleanness respectively. Vishnu was lying on a huge snake and flowing on sea. From his belly button grew a lotus on which Brahmadeva was sitting. Usually, he is mild, but once gets angry, he would be very horrible. Garuda bird, a redpoll, is the ride of Vishnu.

According to *Bhagavata Purana*, Vajravarahi is one of trans formation of Vishnu, who has ten important transformations, the other nine are the fish, turtle, wild boar, lion man dwarf, parasurama, rama, mahakala, buddha and white horse. A story said that as soon as Vishnu saw Veilniyagoso, the demon making the earth sink into the ocean, Vishnu transformed himself as a wild boar and dived into the ocean to pull the earth out. Another saying is that his Dharanibharya, who appeared as a wild boar, was taken into Buddhism as a dharma protector and belongs to the lokuttara dakini. In the Buddhist theory, the lokuttara dakini is the basis of emptiness and happiness and the source of success. The reason that Vajravarahi is regarded as the transformation of Vairochana

金刚亥母单身像

The Single-body Statue of Vajravarahi

金刚亥母是空和乐的根本，一切成就之源。由于毗湿奴具有的太阳神属性，在密教里，金刚亥母被看成是毗卢遮那佛（大日如来）的化身。

藏文版《莲花生大师本生传》中有马头金刚和金刚亥母降伏恶魔的传说：当印度教的恶魔茹扎破坏佛法时，度母化现金刚亥母，观世音菩萨化现马头金刚，降落到喜马拉雅山顶，共同降伏恶魔，马头金刚嘶鸣三声，金刚亥母怒叫五声，并跳起金刚舞步以威慑茹扎。可是，茹扎不但不怕，反而毫不在乎地朝马头金刚和金刚亥母叫嚣。马头金刚大怒，钻入恶魔的腹中，从其头顶探出马头，手脚不停地踢打。金刚亥母钻进恶魔妻子的体内，从其头顶露出猪首。其他诸佛、护法神也一起进入恶魔腹内，恶魔疼痛难忍，只好求饶。

金刚亥母形象较多，据不完全统计，共有九种，常见的有单身和双身两种形象。单身一面二臂像，双唇合闭，两眼、眉毛细长，额上一眼竖起，面目清秀，慈祥和蔼。她头戴五骷髅冠，上竖的发髻上端有一猪头，象征大痴法界体性智；颈挂五十颗骷髅串成的项链；双耳戴铃形耳环；璎珞满身，用一小铃花朵做装饰，婀娜多姿；左手托着盛

is that Vishnu has the attribution of Sun God.

A story about Hayagriva and Vajravarahi in *Biography of Padmasambhava* describes that there was a time when Ru-Dra, a Hinduism demon, ruined Buddhism, Tara and Avalokitesvara got together to fight against Ru-Dra. They made use of their superpowers to transform themselves as Vajravarahi and Hayagriva. Although Hayagriva made three whinny sounds and Vajravarahi performed the vajra dance, Ru-Dra was not only fearless, but also challenged them. Hayagriva was so furious that he got into the demon's abdomen and tore his head and beat him without stop. Vajravarahi also entered into the abdomen of the demon's wife and impaled her head. Seeing this, other dharma protectors all crowded into the demon's abdomen. Ru-Dra could not bear the pain, he had no choice but to beg for mercy.

According to statistics, the images of Vajravarahi approximately comprise of nine kinds. Among them, the single-body and the double-body are normal. The single-body image of her has one face and two arms. Usually, she closes her mouth. In the middle of her long and thin eyes and eyebrows is her third erecting eye. She has a delicate and amiable face. She wears a five-skull crown, beside which there is a wild boar's head which means Great Fool Intelligence as the Fundamental Nature of the Dharmadhatu. Her neck wears a fifty-skull necklace, her big long ears wear bell-like earrings. Various jewelries decorate her body that make her body looks beautiful. The bloody skull container held in her left hand is the symbol of gaining the experience of great happiness. A skull cane hugged by her left elbow symbolizes Dharmakaya, Sambhogakaya and Nirmanakaya. On the top of the cane was decorated a skull, a

金刚亥母忿怒相

The Wrathful Appearance of Vajravarahi

满鲜血的颅器置于胸前，象征获得了大乐体验；左臂夹着法、报、化三身骷髅杖幡，骷髅杖幡上端有骷髅、干枯人头和新鲜人头，下端按压仰卧恶魔，象征压服了贪、嗔、痴三毒的侵扰；右手高举智慧钺刀，象征断除一切烦恼，召引智慧真性；右腿弯曲悬空，脚尖朝下；左腿立姿，足踩一仰卧婆罗门教徒，表示战胜一切异教徒。

金刚亥母忿怒相，怒发呈火焰状，发髻右边有一猪头，三目圆睁，怒目而视，张嘴露出獠牙，十分恐怖；其头饰和项饰同寂静相；丰乳细腰；右手举钺刀，左手托嘎巴拉碗，肘弯中夹着喀章嘎杖；单足踩踏一个仰卧的婆罗门神，做出舞立姿态。金刚亥母双身像中，一般金刚亥母都与本尊胜乐金刚相抱。

dry human head and a bloody head. The cane presses a demon, that means she tames the desire, angry and foolish. A knife lifted by her right hand represents cutting off all troubles and gaining wisdom. Her right leg stands on toe. Her left foot steps on a Brahmanist which means overcoming all non-Buddhism.

The wrathful image of Vajravarahi is very horrible. Her angry hair seems to be burning, beside which is the head of the wild boar head. Her three glaring eyes open widely. She opens mouth and exposes her teeth, that makes people feel horrific. Her head decorates the same adornments with her quiet image, the one above. She has big breasts and slender waist. Her right hand lifts a knife and left hand holds a skull container and the left elbow pick up human bones. One of her foot steps on a deity of Prahmin and make a dancing posture. The double-body Vajravarahi usually hugs with Cakrasamvara.

金刚亥母

Vajravarahi

金刚亥母单身像

The Single-body Statue of Vajravarahi

金刚亥母

Vajravarahi

十

马头金刚

Hayagriva

马头金刚
Hayagriva

马头金刚，又称“马头观自在”，梵文为 Hayagriva。藏文为 RTa-mGrin，意为“马项”或“马喉”。他既是修法本尊，又是护法神，在藏区民间具有很高的声望。因为他是观世音菩萨的自性身，六观音之一，所以被看成是胎藏界观世音菩萨院之一尊，以马头置于头，故名“马头观音”。也说他是无量寿佛的忿怒相，为忿怒威猛摧伏之形，故名“马头明王”。关于马头金刚的来源，古印度教有这样的传说：主神梵天创造了天和地、神与鬼，天神与鬼魔屡战不休，天神凭借《吠陀经》赋予的神力屡战屡胜，因此，鬼魔总想着毁掉《吠陀经》，便派了两个魔鬼趁天神熟睡之时，欲盗出《吠陀经》后撕碎，扔进大海。《吠陀经》是众神力量的来源，世界秩序的根本，没有了它，世界会变得一片混乱，而且面临毁灭的境地。这时，毗湿奴化现出马头金刚杀死魔鬼，抢救出《吠陀经》，拯救了世界。由此，马头金刚成了经典知识的保护者，后被佛教吸收成为佛法的保护神。

马头金刚与藏传佛教产生联系始自公元八世纪，被尊为宁玛派祖师的莲花生进藏时带来马头金刚像及其修法，并亲自指导赤松德赞王和其他人修习。宗派出现以后，马头金刚的形象越来越多，内容日趋丰富，宁玛派把他尊为

Hayagriva, RTa-mGrin in Tibetan, means horse neck or horse throat. Hayagriva uses horse head decorating his hair, so he is also be called Hayagriva Avalokiteshvara. Due to Hayagriva is not only the Satyadevata for practicing yoga but also a dharma protector, he enjoys a high reputation in Tibet. Because he is the self-natural body of Avalokiteshvara, Hayagriva is regarded as one of the six transformations of Avalokiteshvara, and as one of the members of the yard of Avalokiteshvara in Garbhadhatu. There is another saying that Hayagriva is the angry appearance of Amitayus Buddha. About the origin of Haygriva, there is a legend in ancient India that after Brahma created the heaven, the earth, the deities and demons, the war between deities and demons were ceaseless. Deities always won the war with the help of *Veda*, so demons always dreamed of destroying *Veda*. One day, two demons stole *Veda* when deities slept deeply. They tore *Veda* in pieces and threw it into the sea. *Veda* is an uncommon book which could give deities the superpower to restore the world in order. Without *Veda*, the world will become a mess and easy to be damaged. At that moment, Vishnu transformed the Hayagriva. Finally, Hayagriva killed demons and rescued the *Veda* and the world. Because of his contribution, Hayagriva became the protector of the classic knowledge, and was then absorbed in Buddhism as dharma protector.

Hayagriva came into Tibet in the 8th century when Padmasambhava, the Father Guru of Nyingma School, came to Tibet to spread Buddhism and brought Hayagriva and its practice method into Tibet. He taught King KHri-Srong-lDe-bTSan and others to practice Hayagriva. After the form of Tibetan Buddhist schools, more and more people practice Hayagriva dharma. As a result, the images of Hayagriva are splendid and meaningful. Nyingma School worships Hayagriva as the Sambhogakaya

马头金刚
Hayagriva

佛的受用身，崇奉有翅膀的马头金刚，格鲁派则以不带翅膀的马头金刚和马头金刚橛为主要供奉对象。

马头金刚的形象较多，最显著的标志是在红色的鬃毛里有一个或三个绿色马头，个别的头顶上还有一条小蛇，膝、手、腕、颈处都盘绕着蛇。常见的马头金刚像有单面三目

of Buddha. And they prefer to worship Hayagriva with wings. However, the Hayagriva worshipped by Geluk School has no wings, they worship the Vajrakilaka of Hayagriva.

Hayagriva has many images, the outstanding feature of which is that there is one or three green horse heads in his red hair. Sometimes, on his hair, there is also a little snake. And his neck, hands, wrists and knees are all coiled by snakes. Normally,

马头金刚双身像

The Double-body Statue of Hayagriva

二臂、六臂和八臂，都是忿怒相，重要标志是小马头仰天长啸。

唐代著名学者一行的《大日经疏》卷五说："诃耶揭唎婆，译云马头，其身非黄非赤，如日初出之色。以白莲华为璎珞等，庄严其身，光焰猛盛，赫奕如鬘。指甲长利，双牙上出，首髻狮子顶毛，作极吼怒之状，此是莲华部忿怒持明王也，犹如转轮王，宝马巡历四洲，于一时一切处，去心不息，诸菩萨大精进力，亦复如是，所以得如是威猛之势，于生死重障中不顾身命，多所摧伏者，正为白净大悲心故，故用白莲璎珞而自严身也。"

一面二臂的马头金刚，二臂象征智慧与慈悲双运。他是佛，也是菩萨，还是护法。因为是护法，所以他成为莲花部的明王。他的身体是红色的，三目圆睁，非常凶猛，象征降伏三界恶魔；发须皆红黄上竖，头系五骷髅发鬘，火焰发髻中有马头，面部为红色，呈现忿怒相，象征空性；口大张，獠牙切齿，似在怒吼，表示摧毁一切无明业障造成的恐怖，会因此现形；耳朵上挂着大耳环，颈上挂着人头串成的项链；右手持骷髅宝杖，左手施期剋印；以虎皮为裙，以蛇为装饰；右腿微屈，左腿伸直，以莲花日轮为座，

Hayagriva has one angry face with three eyes. There are images of two arms, six arms and eight arms, the most remarkable feature of which is the horse standing on head and howling to the sky.

In Tang Dynasty a famous Buddhist scholar, named Yi Xing, said in *Commentary on Mahavairochana Sutra* that, Hayagriva, means horse head, is the color that neither yellow nor red, like the color of sunrise. His body is decorated by the ornaments of white lotus. His body looks very brave likes burning fire. His nails very long and hard likes sword. His teeth are exposed from mouth. He has lion-like hair style, looks like making a lion roar. He is an angry vidyaraja of Padma Family. He travels Four Continents as if a Chakravartiraja riding a precious horse, do not stay any places, just like other great studious Bodhisattvas. So Hayagriva gets the mighty power to conquer lots of obstacles from birth to death without hesitation for a moment. Because of his pure and great compassion, he is decorated by waist chains made by white lotuses.

One-head and two-arm Hayagriva is not only Buddha, but also Bodhisattva and the dharma protector. As a dharma protector, he is the Protector of the Vidyaraja of Padma Family. He had a red body and red yellow hair with a green horse head on it and a crown with five skulls on his hair. He wears big earrings on his ears and human-head necklace on his neck. His three eyes open widely, that makes him very horrible, and means taming demons in three worlds. While his two tusks expose out of mouth, as if he is roaring, which means when destroying all fears generated by obstacle of ignorance, he makes an appearance. He holds a skull cane in the right hand, while his left hand makes a Tarjani mudra. The two arms symbols wisdom and compassion. A tiger-skirt is

一头二臂马头金刚
One-head and Two-arm Hayagriva

威然立于炽热般若烈焰中；肩披象皮、人肠绳，以蛇缠身，象征镇压龙王。

一头四臂马头金刚，身体为棕红色，火焰形的发髻中有三个马头，似在仰头嘶鸣；头冠、项饰、耳饰等和二臂马头金刚相同；左肩有一长蛇系于肩上；腰系虎皮裙；右边上手持金刚杵，下手持钺刀；左边上手持莲花，下手持金翅鸟；左腿伸展，脚踏长蛇；右腿微屈，象征降伏了烦恼、蕴、天、死四魔。

三头六臂像比较少见，其一头居中（正面），左右各有一头，中间一面为红色，左面为白色，右面为青灰色；火焰发髻中有三个马头，中间的头的面朝前，其他二头的面朝左右两个方向，做出张口嘶鸣状，表示向天界、空界、地界挑战；头系五骷髅鬘，耳环硕大，颈挂人头项链；六臂在身体的两侧呈扇形，其中左右主臂拥抱红色的多罗明妃，手分别持金刚铃和金刚杵，象征方便和智慧，其余四手拿嘎巴拉碗、绳索、蛇、骷髅杖等。也有不抱明妃的，右边第一只手上扬，或施期剋印，其余五只手分别持金刚杵、羂索、骷髅杖、宝剑和颅器。此外，该像还足踏群蛇或恶魔。

tied on his waist with a snake ornament. His right leg bends a little, left leg is straightened. He stands on a lotus seat with burning fire around him. An elephant skin and a rope made by human intestine hang on his shoulders, several snakes twine around his body, all these means he success in suppressing dragon king.

The image of Hayagriva with one head and four arms has brownish red body. His fire-like style hair has three horse-head ornaments, these horse heads vividly roar toward the heaven. He wears the same crown, earrings and necklace with the two-arm Hayagriva. A long snake ties on his left shoulder, a tiger-skin skirt ties on his waist. The two right hands hold a vajra and curved knife, and the two left hands hold a lotus and a garuda bird. His left leg straightens and steps on a long snake, his right leg bend a little which means he has tamed Four Demons, such as Afflictions Demon, Aggregates Demon, Deva Demon and Death Demon.

The three-head and six-arm image of Hayagriva is rare. His middle face is red, the left is white and the right is gray. On the red fire-like hair, there are three horse heads which represent that he challenges the world of heaven, the world of emptiness and the world of earth. He also wears a five-skull crown, a pair of huge earrings and a human-head necklace. The main pair of arms hugs the dakini of Tara and holds a vajra bell and a vajra in hands which mean method and wisdom. The rest of the hands hold a skull bowl, a rope, a snake and a skull cane respectively. But there are the three-head and six-arm Hayagriva without hugging Tara. His right first hand makes a Tarjani mudra, which means eliminating evil obstacles. The rest five hands holds a vajra, a rope, a skeleton cane, a sword, a skull container. He stands on the snakes and demons.

三头六臂马头金刚

Three-head and Six-arm Hayagriva

三头六臂马头金刚

Three-head and Six-arm Hayagriva

一头二臂马头金刚

One-head and Two-arm Hayagriva

马头金刚不仅是降伏罗刹、恶魔等一切魔障，保护佛法弘扬的护法神，而且也是消除旱灾、水患、瘟疫、病魔，救度众生的本尊佛。此外，在藏密中，还有不同的马头金刚造像，一般称为密相马头金刚。《马头金刚仪轨》写到："红色三头共六臂，中红右绿左白脸，上有马头翠绿色，怒啸震慑众邪魔，右持金杵尸杖剑，左手持印矛肠绳，表情愤怒具九相，尸林装束具八足，左伸右屈踩八蟒，周围熊熊烈火烧，体肉从喉至足跟，密布微尘金刚身。"

Hayagriva is not only the dharma protector who subdues demons and protects Buddhism, but also the Satyadevata who brings luck to the living beings, eliminates natural disasters, such as droughts, floods and pestilences, and gives a hand to people. Besides, it is said in *the Rite of Hayagriva* that Hayagriva has three red heads and six arms. His middle face is red, the right face, green and the left face, white. The horse head above the middle face is green and roars to suppress evils and demons. He holds a sword in his right hand and a rope in his left hand. He has eight angry look, wears Corpse Cemeteries' clothes. He has eight feet, each of them steps on a python. Burning fire is around him. Atoms cover his vajra body from throat to feet.

大白伞盖佛母

Sitatapata Buddhamatri

大白伞盖佛母曼荼罗

The Mandala of Sitatapata Buddhamatri

附录

Appendix

重点词汇

Satyadevata 本尊

Tibetan Esoteric Buddhism 藏传密宗

Indian Esoteric Buddhism 印度密教

Han Buddhism 汉传佛教

The Union of Tribes of Yar-Klungs-sPur-rGyal 雅隆悉补野部落联盟

Padma Family 莲花部

Kriyatantra 事部

Charyatantra 行部

Yogacharya 瑜伽部

Anuttara Yoga 无上瑜伽部

Mahasampanna 大圆满

Bon Religion 苯教

Vajrayana 金刚乘

Secrets of Vairochana 集密

Yamantaka 大威德

Hevajra 喜金刚

Samvara 胜乐

Kalacakra 时轮

Nyingma School 宁玛派

Kadam School 噶当派

Sakya School 萨迦派

Kagyu School 噶举派

Jonangpa School 觉囊派

Sixteen Bindus 十六明点

Margaphala 道果教授

Mahamudra 大手印

Six-branch Yoga　六支瑜伽

Mahakala　大黑天

Hayagriva　马头金刚

Acala　不动明王

Lakshmi　吉祥天母

Kalacakra Vajra　时轮金刚

Cakrasamvara　胜乐金刚

Guhyasamaja　集密金刚

Vajrabhairava　大威德金刚

Deity of Nyenchen Tanglha Mountain　念青唐古拉山神

Spirit of Vajrapani　金刚手菩萨的精魂

Deities of Five Longevous Sisters　长寿五姐妹

Dakini　空行佛母

Vajra Dakini　金刚空行母

Ratna Dakini　宝空行母

Padma Dakini　莲花空行母

Karma Dakini　业力空行母

Acala Lakshmi　不动金刚吉祥佛母

Vajra Krodhikali　金刚忿怒母

Vajrahasa Mother　金刚笑母

Vajra Devakanya Sambhogakaya Mother　金刚天女受用母

Vajranrityani　金刚舞女

Mandala　曼荼罗

Tan City　坛城

Maha Mandala　大曼荼罗

Samaya Mandala　三昧耶曼荼罗

Dharma Mandala　法曼荼罗

Karma Mandala　羯磨曼荼罗

Garbhadhatu Mandala 胎藏界曼荼罗

Vajradhatu Mandala 金刚界曼荼罗

Eight-leaves Lotus Yard 八叶莲花院

Universal Knowledge Yard 遍知院

Shakya Yard 释迦院

Manjushri Yard 文殊院

Vajrapani Yard 金刚手院

Sarvanivara Naviskambini Yard 除盖障院

Vidyadhara Yard 持明院

Akashagarbha Yard 虚空藏院

Susiddhi Yard 苏悉地院

Avalokitesvara Yard 观音院

Kshitigarbha Yard 地藏院

Thunderbolt Class Yard 金刚部院

Buddha Family 如来部

Vajra Family 金刚部

Treasure Family 宝部

Dharma Family 法部

Karma Family 羯磨部

Mahavairochana Buddha 大日如来佛

Akshobhya Buddha 不动金刚佛

Ratnasambhava Buddha 宝生佛

Amitabha Buddha 阿弥陀佛

Amoghasiddhi Buddha 不空成就佛

Tangka 唐卡

Samantabhadra Buddha 普贤佛

Truthful Mind 真实意

Vajrakilaka 金刚橛

Sweet Dew Merits 甘露功德

Lotus Word 莲花语

Eight Dharma Actions 八大法行

Supreme Yoga Tantra 无上瑜伽密法

Kalacakra Six-branch Yoga 时轮六支瑜伽

The Union of Shamatha and Vipashyana 止观双运

Vajravarahi 金刚亥母

Vajrapani 金刚手

Vajradhara 金刚持

Mahakalpa 劫（印度时间单位）

Abhisheka 灌顶

Three Realms 三界

Vajra Bell 金刚铃

Vajra 金刚杵

Akanishta 色究竟天

Dharmakaya 法身

Sambhogakaya 报身

Nirmanakaya 化身

All Living Beings 众生

Bodhi Mind 菩提心

Manjushri 文殊

Avalokitesvara 观世音

Kshitigarbha 地藏

Sarvanivara Naviskambini 除盖障

Akashagarbha 虚空藏

Samantabhadra 普贤

Maitreya 弥勒

Living Beings 有情众生

External Wheel of Time 外时轮

Internal Wheel of Time 内时轮

Other Wheel of Time 别时轮

The Realm of Matter 器世间

The Realm of Feeling 情世间

Qi 气

Meridian 脉

Bindu 明点

Shambala 香巴拉

Gridhrakuta Mountain 灵鹫山

Language Ishvara of Dharmadhatu 法界语自在

Body 身

Mouth 语

Mind 意

Mandala of Lucky Stars 吉祥星宿曼荼罗

Devas 天

Nagas 龙

Yakshas 夜叉

Sum-Ba Ye-SHes-dPal ‘Byor 松巴·益西班觉

King Candrabhadra 月贤王

Malaya Garden 玛拉雅花园

Dajra Vehicle 金刚乘

The Teaching of Kalacakrathe 时轮教法

Kalapa 伽拉巴

Suryaprabha 日光

Usnisavijaya 尊胜天女

Vajradharapona 伐折罗波那

Sridanayataka 室利达那耶陀迦

Bhyamyujyate 具种

Mahakalachakrapada 大时轮足

Sirtha River 悉多河

World of Holding Happiness 持乐世界

Sukhavati World 极乐世界

The Wish-fulfilling Lake 如意湖

The White Lotus Lake 白莲湖

Cakravartin 转轮王

Yojana 由旬（印度长度单位）

Sambhogakaya Buddha 报身佛

Buddhamatri 佛母

Buddhavamsa 佛陀种性

Prajna Buddhamatri 智慧佛母

Ten Paramitas 十波罗蜜多

Alms Giving 布施

Keep Moral Laws 持戒

Patience Under Insult 忍辱

Pure Progress 精进

Meditation 禅定

Wisdom 智慧

Skillful method 方便

Wishes 愿

Strength 力

Knowledge 智

Indra 因陀罗

Brahmadeva 梵天

Shiva 湿婆

Mahesvara 大自在天

Yama 阎摩

Rupadhatu 色界

Eighting Loka of Rupathatu 色界十八天

Dharma of Samvara 胜乐法

Sumeru Mount 须弥山

Jambudvipa 南瞻部洲

Tushita 兜率

Mountain of Dhanakataka 驮那羯傑迦山

Samvara Samadhi　胜乐三摩地

The wrathful Appearance of Cakrasamvaras　胜乐本尊忿怒相

Rudra　楼陀罗

Dushkara Charya　苦行（之）神

Lord of Dancing　舞蹈（之）神

Total Holding Wheel　总摄轮

Dakini Fredom　空行自在

Vajra Wheel　金刚轮

Brave Vajra　英勇金刚

Moon Crown　月冠冕

Possessing Bliss　有福

Mother Tantras　母续

Quarrel Kalpa Era　诤劫时

Four Kalpa Eras　四劫时

Trisection Kalpa Era　三分劫时

Bisection Kalpa Era　二分劫时

Perfect Kalpa Era　圆满劫时

Eight Big Cemeteries　八大尸林

Eastern Brutal Cemetery　东方暴虐寒林

Northern Jungle Cemetery　北方密丛寒林

Southern Bone Cemetery　南方骨锁寒林

Western Vajra Fire Cemetery　西方金刚焰寒林

North-eastern Laughing Cemetery　东北方狂笑寒林

South-eastern Lucky Cemetery　东南方吉祥寒林

South-western Gloomy Cemetery　西南方幽暗寒林

North-western Twittering Cemetery　西北方啾啾寒林

The Brave Father and Dakinis of Five Family　五部勇父空行

Pravaracakra Samvara　最胜胜乐金刚

Viracakra Samvara　勇士胜乐金刚

Garudacakra Samvara　迦楼罗胜乐金刚

Jatakacakra Samvara 本生胜乐金刚

Sahajacakra Samvara 俱生胜乐金刚

Mani jewel 摩尼宝珠

Mahesvaradevakanya 大自在天女

Dharanibharya 明妃

Boundless Kindness 慈无量心

Boundless Compassion 悲无量心

Boundless Joy 喜无量心

Limitless Impartiality 舍无量心

Increasing 增益

Twelve Dependent Origination 十二缘起

Ignorance 无明

Action 行

Consciousness 识

Name and form 名色

Six Senses 六识

Contact 触

Thirst 爱

Grasp 取

Becoming 有

Born 生

Aging and Death 老死

Krsnayaksnini 黑夜叉女、时间女神

Bhairavamshiva 怖畏湿婆

Heruka 呬噜嘎

Tarjani Gesture 期剋印

Deviuma 邬摩天女

Mudra Gesture 手印

Big Happiness Wheel 大乐轮

Black Mind Wheel 黑色意轮

Red Language Wheel 红色语轮

Moon-like Color Body Wheel 净如月亮的身轮

Dharma Instrument 法器

Mandra 真言咒语

Arising Orderly 生起次第

Perfecting Orderly 圆满次第

Observation 观想

Yogini 瑜伽母

Homa 护摩

Yogini Tantra 瑜伽母续

Devikali 迦梨

Triple-thousand worlds 三千世界

Vinayaka King 毗那夜迦王

Sannayaka King 扇那夜迦王

Subhakarasimha 善无畏

Ganapati 欢喜天

Anatman 无我

Four Demons 四魔

Afflictions Demon 烦恼魔

Aggregates Demon 蕴魔

Deva Demon 天魔

Death Demon 死魔

Samahita 等引

Single-body Statue 单身像

Double-body Statue 双身像

Aksobhyavajra Buddha 不动金刚佛

Amitabha Buddha 阿弥陀佛

Vairocana Buddha 毗卢遮那佛

Vajrapasha Bodhisattva Dakini 明妃金刚锁菩萨

Petari Dakini 贝塔莉空行母

Juntari Dakini　军荼莉空行母

Dongbi Dakini　东比空行母

Five Aggregates　五蕴

Four Elements　四大

Heri Dakini　诃黎空行母

Kesimarui Dakini　葛斯玛瑞空行母

Gori Dakini　高黎空行母

Sawarui Dakini　沙瓦瑞空行母

Bukakasi Dakini　布嘎嘎斯空行母

The body of illusion and transformation　幻化身

Amitayus Buddha　无量寿佛

Arupadhatu　无色界

Kamadhatu　欲界

Trayastrimshas　三十三天

Vishnu　遍入天、毗湿奴

Asura　阿修罗

Ultimate Truth　胜义谛

Worldly Truth　世俗谛

Rolangma　金刚露漩

Samsara　轮回

Moha Yamantaka　痴阎摩敌

Matsarya Yamantaka　悭阎摩敌

Kama Yamantaka　贪阎摩敌

Irsya Yamantaka　妒阎摩敌

Ayoghana Yamantaka　锤阎摩敌

Salaka Yamantaka　杖阎摩敌

Padma Yamantaka　莲花阎摩敌

Astra Yamantaka　剑阎摩敌

Father Tantra　父续

Sravaka　声闻

Raksa　罗刹

Sarasvat　妙音天女

Dipamkara Buddha　燃灯佛

Devakany　天女

The Tathagata of Great Moni King　大摩尼珠王如来

Soha World　娑婆世界

Dragon King　龙王

Yaksa　药叉

Tara　度母

Vidyaraja　明王

Garuda Bird　金翅鸟

Lha-THo-Tho-Ri-sNYan-bTSan　拉脱脱日年赞

THon-Mi-Sam-BHo-Ta　吞米桑布扎

Srong-bTSan-sGam-Po　松赞干布

KHri-Srong-lDe-bTSan　赤松德赞

KHri-lDe-Srong-bTSan　赤德松赞

KHri-gTShug-lDe-bTSan　赤祖德赞

SMan-GHang-Lugs　勉唐

MKHyen-bTSe' i-Lugs　钦孜

SGar-bRis-Lugs　噶赤

The Sutra of Ornament of the mahayana of the Great King　《佛说大乘庄严宝王经》

The Sutra of Hundreds Kowtow and Penitence　《百拜忏悔经》

The Six-Syllable Tantra　《六字大明陀罗尼》

Hevajra Fundamental Tantra　《喜金刚本续》

Kalacakra Fundamental Tantra　《时轮根本续》

Mahavairochana Sutra　《大日经》

Vajrashekhara Sutra　《金刚顶经》

Samvara Fundamental Tantra　《胜乐根本续》

Guhyasamaja Fundamental Tantra　《集密根本续》

The Wisdom Sutra 《般若经》

History of Kokonor 《如意宝树史》

Records of Tibetan Kings and Ministers 《西藏王臣记》

The Fundamental Tantra of Kalacakra of Lucky First Buddha 《吉祥最初佛时轮金刚根本续》

The Wide Commentary on the Fundamental Tantra of Kalacakra Vajra 《金刚根本续广疏》

Three Bodhisattva Commentary 《三菩萨释》

The First Extraordinary Buddha Fundamental Tantra of Kalacakra 《时轮根本续殊胜最初佛》

Kalacakra ' s Origin and Source 《时轮源流》

The Biography of RGyal-dPalGrags-Pa 《坚华扎巴传》

The Guide to Shambhala 《香巴拉指南》

The Rules and Ceremonies of Dakini ' s Net 《空行母网律仪》

Veda Sutra 《吠陀经》

The Commentary of Wisdom of Kalacakra Mulagrantha Tantra 《时轮根本续·智慧品释》

Great Holy Joy Offering Ritual 《大圣欢喜供养法》

The Rules and Ceremonies of Hevajra and Dakini ' s Illusory Net 《喜金刚空行母幻网律仪轨》

The Collection of Auspicious Hevajra's Dew Spring 《吉祥喜金刚集轮甘露泉》

The Tantra of Six-face Child 《六面童子续》

The Tantra of Yamantaka 《阎摩德迦续》

The Tantra of Yamantaka ' s Black Enermy 《阎摩德迦黑敌续》

The Tantra of Nine Yamantakas 《九尊大威德续》

The Dharma of Yamantaka ' s Origin and Source 《大威德教法源流》

The Origin and Source of Yamantaka Teaching 《阎摩德迦教法源流》

The Origin and Source of Auspicious Vajrabhairava's Teaching: Successors in Three Worlds 《吉祥大威德金刚教法源流——三界尊胜成就库品》

The Successive Method of Practicing Auspicious Vajrabhairava 《吉祥大金刚怖畏生起次第安立显耀顶饰》

The Sutra of Great Lakshmi 's One Hundred and Eight Names 《佛说大吉祥天女十二契一百八名无垢大乘经》

The Sutra of the Great Lakshmi 's Twelve Names 《大吉祥天女十二名号经》

Rig Veda 《梨俱吠陀》

Brahmana 《梵书》

Atharva Veda 《阿闼婆吠陀》

The Tantra of Buddha said Mahakala's Great Merit and Perfect Bodhisattva 《佛说摩诃迦罗大黑天神大福德自在圆满菩萨陀罗尼经》

Deities, Ghosts and Monsters in Tibet 《西藏的神灵和鬼怪》

Manu Smriti 《摩奴法典》

Bhagavata Purana 《薄伽梵往世书》

Biography of Padmasambhava 《莲花生大师本生传》

Commentary on Mahavairochana Sutra 《大日经疏》

The Rite of Hayagriva 《马头金刚仪轨》

作者简介 **索南才让（许德存）** 青海乐都人。现为西藏民族大学教授，为国务院特殊津贴享受者、新世纪“百千万人才工程”国家级人选等。长期从事教学和研究工作，主要研究方向为宗教哲学、藏族历史与文化，著、译有《西藏密教史》等二十多部，发表学术论文九十余篇。主持参与国家社科基金项目十项（其中重大项目四项）、教育部项目两项、国家民委项目两项等。

Pro. BSod Nams TSHe Ring, or Xu Decun, was born in Ledu county of Qinghai province, now is working for Xizang Minzu University. He is a receiver of Special Allowance from the State Council, a talent of National Candidate for the New Century Talents Project, and so on.He has engaged in teaching and research for a long time, and has made certain achievements in religious philosophy, Tibetan history and culture. He published several works, such as *Tibetan Esoteric History*, and more than 20 books. Besides, he still published more than 90 academic papers, and leaded and participated in ten projects of the National Social Science Fund (including four major projects), two projects from the Ministry of Education, two projects from the National Ethnic Affairs Commission, and many other scientific research projects.

译者简介 **顾毳** 贵阳学院阳明学与黔学研究院副教授，主要研究方向为藏传佛教哲学。出版译著《印度佛教后期“空有融合”思想佛论选译》（藏译汉），发表学术论文数篇。

Dr. Gu Cui, is an associate professor in Institute of Yangmingism and Qianism of Guiyang University. Her main studying is Tibetan Buddhist philosophy, published the selected translation of Buddhist treatises about the Fusing Mādhyamika and Vijñaptimātra and several academic articles.

本书供稿 北京中和明德文化传播有限责任公司

图书代号：SK21N0633

图书在版编目（CIP）数据

藏密本尊 : 汉英对照 / 索南才让著 . — 西安 :
陕西师范大学出版总社有限公司 , 2021.3
ISBN 978-7-5695-1744-6

Ⅰ . ①藏… Ⅱ . ①索… Ⅲ . ①喇嘛宗—画册
Ⅳ . ① B946.6-64

中国版本图书馆 CIP 数据核字 (2020) 第 122179 号

藏密本尊（汉英对照）

ZANG MI BENZUN（HAN-YING DUIZHAO）

索南才让 著　　顾彝 译

出版统筹 刘东风　郭永新
选题策划 来新国　王文成
责任编辑 陈柳冬雪
特约编辑（中文） 秦　丹　孟淑贤
特约编辑（英文） 乌　炜　索瑞娅　王晶晶
特约编辑（图片） 王晶晶　乌　琛
编　　务 尹　楠
责任校对 尹海宏
装帧设计 雅昌设计中心 · 北京
内文制作 龙山文化
出版发行 陕西师范大学出版总社
（西安市长安南路 199 号　邮编 710062）
网　　址 http://www.snupg.com
印　　制 北京雅昌艺术印刷有限公司
开　　本 889 mm × 1194 mm　1/12
印　　张 19
插　　页 4
字　　数 166 千
版　　次 2021 年 3 月第 1 版
印　　次 2021 年 3 月第 1 次印刷
书　　号 ISBN 978-7-5695-1744-6
定　　价 360.00 元

读者购书、书店添货或发现印装质量问题，请与本公司营销部联系、调换。
电话：（029）85307864　85303629　传真：（029）85303879